A volume in the Hyperion reprint series
PIONEERS OF THE WOMAN'S MOVEMENT

HYPERION PRESS, INC.
Westport, Connecticut

THE

SEXES THROUGHOUT NATURE

BY

ANTOINETTE BROWN BLACKWELL

Author of " Studies in General Science," &c., &c

NEW YORK
G. P. PUTNAM'S SONS
FOURTH AVENUE AND TWENTY-THIRD STREET
1875

Published in 1875 by G.P. Putnam's Sons, New York
Hyperion reprint edition 1976
Library of Congress Catalog Number 75-7714
ISBN 0-88355-349-X
Printed in the United States of America

Library of Congress Cataloging in Publication Data

Blackwell, Antoinette Louisa Brown, 1825-1921.
   The sexes throughout nature.

   (Pioneers of the woman's movement)
   Reprint of the ed. published by Putnam, New York.
   1. Sex. 2. Women — Social and moral questions.
I. Title.
HQ21.B63   1976   301.41'2   75-7714
ISBN 0-88355-349-X

PREFACE.

————

IN the present volume, the leading Essay—*Sex and Evolution*—and the concluding Paper—*The Trial by Science*—are for the first time offered to the public.

Of the briefer articles, that on *The Alleged Antagonism between Growth and Reproduction*, appeared first in the *Popular Science Monthly*. The others, now slightly modified and rearranged, were first published in numbers in the *Woman's Journal*.

These essays, closely related in subject, are all hung upon a framework of criticism. The great names of the gentlemen whose positions are controverted, as the oak to the ivy, serve as an excellent support to the overgrowing theses. Moreover, it is easier to pull down than to build up ; yet I have earnestly attempted to do something of both.

Many women have grievously felt the burden of laws or customs interfering unwarrantably with their property, their children, or their political and personal rights. I have felt this also ; but more than any or all other forms of limitation and proscription, I have realized in my inmost soul that most subtle outlawry of the feminine intellect which warns it off from the highest fields of human research. But now arises a question which—taken away from the protection of accepted tradition—is rather unexpectedly thrust forward for purely scientific recognition and settlement. Some of the grandest names known to science have already taken it up for investigation ; but their conclusions are eminently unsatisfactory !

However superior their powers, their opportunities, their established scientific positions, yet in this field of inquiry *pertaining to the normal powers and functions of Woman*, it is they who are at a disadvantage. Whatever else women may not venture to study and explain with authority, on this topic they are more than the peers of the wisest men in Christendom. Experience must have more weight than any amount of outside observation. We are clearly entitled, on this subject, to a respectful hearing.

In this faith, I offer the public these somewhat fragmentary papers; believing that they contain the germs of a new scientific estimate of feminine nature, from its earliest dawning in the plant up to developed womanhood in all its present complexity. They are probably faulty in many things, and may be proved to be wrong even on some very important points. The work is printed as it was written—in snatches—not because the writer would escape the labor of systematic revision, but from the conviction that it will be more acceptable to the general reader in its present form. There are occasional repetitions, but it is believed that each presents the subject in some new phase. The discussions are brief. Many other facts might be given, and many additional points brought forward in evidence of the main positions. But perhaps the book is quite long enough as it is.

The whole line of thought must submit, like all

other reasoning, to be tested by the accumulation of pertinent facts which will either expose its fallacies or furnish its final justification.

THE AUTHOR.

CONTENTS.

SEX AND EVOLUTION.

THE STATEMENT.

IT is the central theory of the present volume that the sexes in each species of beings compared upon the same plane, from the lowest to the highest, are always true equivalents—equals but not identicals in development and in relative amounts of all normal force. This is an hypothesis which must be decided upon the simple basis of fact.

If the special class of feminine instincts and tendencies is a fair offset in every grade of life to corresponding masculine traits, this is a subject for direct scientific investigation. It is a question of pure quantity; of comparing unlike but strictly measurable terms. In time it can be experimentally decided, and settled by rigidly mathematical tests. We do not weigh lead and sunbeams in the same balance; yet the *savants* can estimate their equivalent forces on some other basis than avoirdupois. So if the average female animal is the natural equiva-

lent of the average male of its own type in the whole
aggregate of their differentiated qualities, science, by
turning concentrated attention to this problem, and
applying the adequate tests, can yet demonstrate this
fact beyond controversy.

Or if the male is everywhere the established
superior, then science in time can undoubtedly
affirm that truth upon a basis of such careful and
exact calculation that every opponent must learn to
acquiesce.

But the question is still very far from reaching
the point of accurate solution. It is decided on both
sides by inferences drawn from, yet untested data.

Nor is it in any way dependent upon the hypothesis of Evolution or upon any phase of that
hypothesis. The leopard and the leopardess either
are or are not mathematical equivalents when fairly
estimated as to all their powers and capacities,
physical and psychical. No question as to their
origin or their mode of growth can affect that
equation.

But each writer can best treat of any subject
from his own standpoint, and hence, in the present

paper, the equivalence of the sexes is considered in the light of certain theories of development.

Mr. Spencer and Mr. Darwin, the accredited exponents of Evolution, are both constructive reasoners. Each, with a special line of investigation, is intent upon the unfolding of related facts and conclusions; and every fresh topic is destined to be examined as to its bearing upon the central points of *the system.*

Any positive thinker is compelled to see everything in the light of his own convictions. The more active and dominant one's opinions, the more liable they must be to modify his rendering of related facts —roping them inadvertently into the undue service of his theories. Add to this the immense concentrated work which both these famous investigators have undertaken for years past, and one may readily understand that on certain points to which they have not given special attention, these great men may be equally liable with lesser ones to form mistaken judgments. When, therefore, Mr. Spencer argues that women are inferior to men because their development must be earlier arrested by reproductive functions, and Mr. Darwin claims that males have evolved muscle and brains much superior to females, and entailed their pre-eminent qualities chiefly on their male descendants, these conclusions need not be accepted without question, even by their own school of evolutionists.

Men see clearly and think sharply when their sympathies are keenly enlisted, but not otherwise. But neither of these high authorities evinces the least vital interest in the dogma of male superiority. Smaller men, who are not pre-eminent over the majority of their own sex, might glory in the relative inferiority of the other. But here there seems to be but small temptation to narrow-mindedness. They accept the theory as a foregone conclusion. Of course they are bound to regard it philosophically when it is thrust upon their attention, and to ground it, like every other fact, upon a common scientific basis. But they both content themselves by pushing forward a few stones of strength, wedging them hastily into their places as underpinning, and leaving them there without being welded together by the cement of long and intent thinking. It is the more annoying therefore, that we should be called on to accept their conclusions on this point, because of their great authority in closely related departments to which they have given almost exclusive attention.

When " Social Statics " was written, Mr. Spencer had some belief in the equivalence of the sexes. Reverting to First Principles, he became so intent on evolving a *system,* that *woman's place in nature* fell out of perspective in his thoughts. The subject must have seemed of too little importance to require long and laborious investigation. The four weighty volumes of Biology and Psychology all indicate that his attention was absorbed elsewhere ; but in a line often running so marvellously near to that of the relation of the sexes, as affected by evolution, that he very narrowly missed giving it his fullest recognition.

In a subsequent paper on the " Psychology of the Sexes," Mr. Spencer does give us a strong, clearly-lined statement of his position ; but the further exposition of it is brief and, for him, only feebly sustained. Now, as Mr. Spencer never yet woke up to any topic around which he was not able to recognize a thousand side considerations, all tending to special modifications of the main conclusion, it is apparent that he has not yet aroused his energies to an adequate consideration of this question.   It is analogically certain that, otherwise, he never would have attempted to crowd the discussion into half-a-dozen brief pages.

Mr. Darwin, also, eminently a student of organic structures, and of the causes which have produced them, with their past and present characters, has failed to hold definitely before his mind the principle that the difference of sex, whatever it may consist in, must itself be subject to *natural selection* and to evolution.   Nothing but the exacting task before him of settling the Origin of all Species and the Descent of Man, through all the ages, could have prevented his recognition of ever-widening organic differences evolved in two distinct lines.   With great wealth of detail, he has illustrated his theory of how the male has probably acquired additional masculine characters ; but he seems never to have thought of looking to see whether or not the females had developed equivalent feminine characters.

The older physiologists not only studied nature

from the male standpoint—as, indeed, they must chiefly, being generally men—but they interpreted facts by the accepted theory that the male is the representative type of the species—the female a modification preordained in the interest of reproduction, and in that interest only or chiefly. To them, physiology was an adjunct of the special creation theory. They believed that Sovereign Power and Wisdom had created one vessel to honor, and the other to dishonor. Evolutionists depart widely from this time-honored basis. But how are we to understand the want of balance in their interpretation of natural methods? It is difficult to perceive what self-adjusting forces, in the organic world, have developed men everywhere the superiors of women, males characteristically the superiors of females.

Other things equal, children of the same parents must begin embryo life on the same plane. As many successive stages of growth have arisen between primordial forms and women, as between these and men. Mr. Spencer reasons, that the cost of reproduction being greater for the female than the male, female development is earlier arrested in pro-

portion.   Hence woman can never equal man, physically or mentally.

Mr. Darwin's theory of Sexual Selection supposes that a male superiority has been evolved in the
male line, and entailed chiefly to the male descendants.   The females, sometimes, inherit characters
originally acquired by the males ; but this form of
evolution is carried forward principally from father to
son, from variety to variety, and from species to
species, beginning with the lowest unisexual beings
and continuing upwards to man.   With a few incon-
siderable exceptions, the more active progressive
male bears off the palm, among all higher animals in
size, and among all animals high and low, in development of muscles, in ornamentation, in general brightness and beauty, in strength of feeling, and in vigor of
intellect.   Weighed, measured, or calculated, the
masculine force always predominates.

Possibly the cause to which Mr. Spencer assigns
the *earlier arrest of feminine development* may be
alleged as the sufficient reason for Mr. Darwin's *male
evolution.*   At any rate, Mr. Spencer scientifically
subtracts from the female, and Mr. Darwin as scien-

tifically *adds to the male.* The inequality between
them is steadily increasing along the whole length of
all the internodes ; and it seems to grow both upwards and downwards, as plants do, from all the
nodes. Unless it meet with a check in some unknown law, the causes which originally superin-
duced the inequality between the sexes must continue to increase it to a degree which it is startling
to contemplate !

These philosophers both believe that inheritance
is limited in a large degree to the same sex, and both
believe in mathematical progression. Where, then, is
male superiority to end ? Are all the races, because
of it, threatened with decadence and death somewhere in the remote future ? Or must the time
arrive when inferior males will be systematically
chosen, and the superior ones thus eliminated from
existence ? But would this be Evolution ? Moreover, if we must fall back upon certain natural checks
which will be able in the future to prevent too great
an inequality between the sexes, it cannot be pre-
posterous to suppose that in the past and in the
present similar natural checks always have been, and

still are, in active operation. These, from the beginning, may have been able, progressively, to maintain a due balance, an approximate equilibrium and equivalence of forces, between the males and females of each species, as it has been successively evolved. To point out the nature of these functional checks, to show that they have produced many various structural modifications in different species, corresponding in each with varying habits and development, but all tending to maintain a virtual equivalence of the sexes, is the aim of the present paper.

The facts of Evolution may have been misinterpreted, by giving undue prominence to such as have been evolved in the male line ; and by overlooking equally essential modifications which have arisen in the diverging female line. It is claimed that average males and females, in every species, always have been approximately equals, both physically and mentally. It is claimed that the extra size, the greater beauty of color, and wealth of appendages, and the greater physical strength and activity in males, have been in each species mathematically offset in the females by corresponding advantages—such as more highly dif-

ferentiated structural development; greater rapidity
of organic processes; larger relative endurance, dependent upon a more facile adjustment of functions
among themselves, thus insuring a more prompt recuperation after every severe tax on the energies.
It is claimed that the stronger passional force in the
male finds its equivalent in the deeper parental and
conjugal affection of the female; and that, in man,
the more aggressive and constructive intellect of the
male, is balanced by a higher intellectual insight,
combined with a greater facility in coping with details and reducing them to harmonious adjustment, in
the female. It is also claimed that in morals—development still modified by the correlative influences
of sex—unlike practical virtues and vices and varied
moral perceptions, must still be regarded as scientific
equivalents.

All characters, being equally transmitted to descendants of both sexes, may remain undeveloped in
either, or may be developed subject to sexual modifications; and yet, as a whole, the males and females
of the same species, from mollusk up to man, may
continue their related evolution, as true equivalents

in all modes of force, physical and psychical.   If this hypothesis can be shown to have a sufficient basis in nature, then Mr. Spencer and Mr. Darwin are both wrong in the conclusion that, in the processes of Evolution, man has become the superior of woman.

I do not underrate the charge of presumption which must attach to any woman who will attempt to controvert the great masters of science and of scientific inference.   But there is no alternative!   Only a woman can approach the subject from a feminine standpoint; and there are none but beginners among us in this class of investigations.   However great the disadvantages under which we are placed, these will never be lessened by waiting.   And are there any who will read this paper, and yet feel that it deals with a class of topics improper for a woman to investigate, and still more unfitting for her to discuss before the public?   Not among men of science, surely; but in the appeal to a popular audience, one may expect to meet some remnant of this sentiment. Then, in the graver phases of relations which may involve modesty, I can but appeal to the old motto of chivalry—*Honi soit qui mal y pense.*   Psychology and physiology are inseparable. Who can escape from the first requisite of knowledge—" know thyself ? "

THE ARGUMENT.

Mr. Spencer reasons that low organisms, with structures that have severally reached their separate limits of evolution, by the union of two cells or perhaps two parts of a cell " slightly differentiated," may effect a " redistribution " of atoms, fitting them to become the basis of a new organism. This explanation is satisfactory. But in the genesis of higher organisms, Mr. Spencer does not fully recognize the growing necessity for *evolution of the differentiation* in primordial cells, in correspondence with more evolved structures and relations. The " slight differentiation," which would suffice to inaugurate an almost homogeneous organism, must be inadequate to so redistribute the forces in two cells of highly complex molecules as to enable their union to evolve the more heterogeneous organism. Hence the evolution of sperm and germ cells must correspond with the evolution of their parent structures.

Their differences must become more highly complex, yet definite in character, in each advancing class. These differences must be so related each to the other that the action of the two will produce just that redistribution of their molecules which is needed to initiate the growth of a new individual of the species to which they are allied. No other re-arrangement will answer.

The pollen which can produce a fertile seed must belong to the same, or at the farthest to an entirely kindred species of plant. Any drop of sap or bit of leaf or stem in contact with the pistil would be "slightly differentiated" from it; yet such indefinite differentiations have never been known to produce the definite result of a perfect seed. But while such a result might not be absolutely impracticable, or at least impossible, on the low plane of plant life, with its community of growth, yet among animals with a distinct individuality and heterogeneity of structure, it would be quite impossible.

On the higher plane, every form of hybridism and all abnormal conditions are restricted within narrow limits. There, far more than lower down in the scale, nature abhors a union too closely kindred, demanding the widest adapted differentiations. The "combinations and antagonisms" of two cells, each of which is a group of incident forces to the other, must have mutual adaptations among themselves, or their union does not result in the new moving equilibrium—a living being. The one group must complement the other in the completed whole.

But adult males and females of every species are differentiated *just in proportion to their general development.* They are evolved not in parallel but in adapted diverging lines. Apparently there exists a definite ratio between the evolution of a species and its sexual divergence. Every detail of each structure becomes somewhat diversely modified, and every function, with its related organs, more definitely unlike its analogue in the opposite sex. In the highest group, the mammals, the sexes differ more widely than with birds or fishes, and these than any class of invertebrates. At the head of the ascending series, men and women are more broadly unlike physiologically and psychologically than any lowe class. This may not be immediately obvious to those who have given but little attention to the subject.

Among certain insects, for example, the two sexes have very unlike forms, and with others they have entirely different habits. Some fungus growths vary their characters with varying external conditions; and among higher plants, such as orchids, three reputed genera have been raised from the same parent. But in this low plane of development, the same sex sometimes has two distinct forms. Insects have been known to have the characters of different species on the two sides of the body. We are forced to conclude that the simpler organisms are more or less indefinite in structure and easily modified by external conditions. Hence we cannot look to these classes for clearly-defined sexual differences.

If we consider *external characters only*, the larger relative size, brighter plumage, and more showy ornaments of male birds distinguish them from their females more obviously than any kindred differences among the mammalia. But when we turn to *the facts of structure and their related modifications in function,* no physiologist can doubt for a moment that wider differences of sex have been evolved in correlation with the general development. These "differentiations" increase in number, and are more elaborately wrought out in detail, extending to slight but well-defined modifications in the whole general system, in addition to becoming more distinctive in primary and secondary sexual characters.

Such differences, less readily noted by the casual observer, are much more fundamentally significant; as the wings of an insect and of a bird may seem to be more kindred organs than the fore-legs of a quadruped with either, though the anatomist decides that the swallow's wings and the horse's fore-legs are almost identical in structure, while the butterfly's wings are not even remotely allied to them in structural plan. Judged by superficial characters, the male and female of the horse would not be highly differentiated; but, deciding according to the fundamental facts of structure and function, this highly-developed species has evolved a corresponding demarcation of sex. This demarcation lies not so much, at least not so obviously, in the differences of bone, and tissue, and nerve, and mental traits—

though all these have been subject to unlike modification—as in *the addition* of exclusively feminine characters.

The insect mother deposits her eggs in a position in which they can find food for themselves as soon as they are hatched, and the hatching process itself is left to the external temperature. The more highly organized bird gives the warmth of her own body to promote the growth of the chick, and she must supply it with food for a long time after it leaves the egg. The mammal, as the horse, gives still more and higher sustenance to its young. And at the head of the scale, the human infant is more dependent on its mother than any other living thing. The male bird may sit on the eggs or " fend for the callow young," but with mammals, corresponding duties are structurally impossible.

The male Pipefish has a pouch into which the young creep for protection. This curious pocket is superficially similar to the analogous structure of female marsupials, but with this characteristic difference, that the Pipefish affords no direct nourishment to his nurselings, while the marsupial assimilates food and injects it into the mouths of her helpless dependents. No male of any species, high or low, is known to afford *direct nutriment* to the young—to first assimilate the food, and then transfer it to the offspring. The nearest approach to this is among pigeons. With these birds, both parents eject half digested food from the crop to feed their young. But there is no female of any species, plant, or animal, which does not in some form elaborate food and effect a direct transfer of it to the seed, the egg, the growing embryo, or the living young. This distinction is universal: *The male never affords direct nurture to offspring; the female always affords direct nurture to offspring.*

Dr. Carpenter, in his "Comparative Physiology," points out the law, that " the higher the grade of development which the being is ultimately to attain, the more is it assisted in the earlier stages by its parent:" showing that the maternal functions are always developed in correspondence with the general development of the species. Let it be noted that the analogous reproductive organs, male and female, are always about equivalent in the same species in com-

plexity of structure and development ; but the related nutritive system, which is exclusively female
and always unique in function, is also evolved in a
definite ratio with all other development.

This system of reproductive nutrition has been
evolved, not in one continuous series, but in several ;
in correspondence with the evolution of species.
The superiority of one mode over another is not
always apparent.   Thus, compare some of the higher
marsupials and the lower placental mammals.
Again, compare some of the larger carnivorous and
herbivorous animals.   The young of the former are
less developed and more feeble at birth, requiring
longer subsequent parental care and protection.   But
the more developed young of the herb-eating mother
has received the greater share of nutrition before
birth.   There is a corresponding development in
both sexes to meet the unlike demand.

The terrestrial carnivora are nearly always mo-
nogamous.   The male forages for the family—that
is, while the female supplies the *direct nurture* of offspring, the male provides largely for their *indirect
nurture.*   Among vegetable-eaters, this division of

labor is impracticable ; then natural selection fixes upon some other division of commensurate duties or acquirements which will be of greatest benefit to the particular species, such as greater beauty of coloring, superior size and strength of muscle, and increased activity of brain. In brief, the evolution of secondary sexual characters developed in the male line, which Mr. Darwin has recognized and followed out extensively, assigning their origin chiefly to sexual selection, we may attribute chiefly to the broader Natural Selection, which, *securing both the survival and the advancement of the fittest, gradually selects secondary or indirect characters which enable average males, equally with average females, to contribute to the general advancement of offspring.*

In nature's division of duties, if the mothers contribute to the direct sustenance of the young, the fathers equally contribute to their indirect sustenance ; or to the advancement of the species in superior attainments, which amounts to the same thing.

It must be a universal law that the evolution of sexual characters, primary or secondary, will extend to corresponding modifications of every molecule in either organism—in re-adjustment of the "moving equilibrium." This principle is another application of Mr. Spencer's statement that variations "once commenced lead, by their combinations and antagonisms, to multiform results." Applied to sex, as to species, "variation is necessitated by the persistence of force."

Genetic elements, uniting, must be of equal values and of equal potency as balanced forces. If the one group be represented by A and the other by B, the fair presumption is that A equals B. If A be supposed to be greater than B, the equilibrium would be much more unstable than in a union of equivalents. An organism grows by the addition of like units, but if the units of A began by being greater than the units of B, this inequality would steadily tend to increase. In time, it might be expected to overthrow the unstable equilibrium.

But if A equalled B, two equivalent adapted groups co-operating, the addition of like elements in the growth of the organism would the more readily maintain the balance in all activities. The action of unequal outside forces in time would doubtless destroy even this more stable equilibrium; yet the advantage gained by the equivalence of the primordial cells would be very great.

But differentiation, to be of practical value, must imply some opposition; unlike tensions or unlike polarities of forces, promoting actions and reactions between the groups. Hence the more nearly the uniting groups are equals and opposites, the greater the initiative power in the new organism. Hence natural selection must tend to promote equivalence in the two classes of primordial cells in each species. Hence natural selection must tend to maintain equivalence in the two sexes of every species, and to carry forward all evolution on two mutually adapted lines.

By the survival of the fittest, the nearest approximations to equivalents in the sexes would leave the greatest number of offspring, and those best adapted to survive. The higher the development of the species and the more differentiated in structure and functions, the greater need would there be of a complex opposite polarity of activities in the uniting elements. Therefore natural selection, acting during immense periods of time, would be able to maintain, through the survival of the fittest, an approximate equality between the sexes at all stages of their development. It would be a differentiated and mutually adjusted equivalence—ultimating in an unlike modification of each which must extend to every function and to every adapted organ, to every thought and action of either sex.

In the inorganic world there is a tendency to the indefinite aggregation of like matter and force. There exist, also, influences which produce an indefinite advance from the homogeneous to the heterogeneous. But in the organic world many definite aggregations, differing in kind or in degree, have been established, each of which tends to perpetuate other aggregates like itself ; yet both the parent organisms and their successors increase in heterogeneity, checked and controlled by certain definite laws.

When like indefinite aggregations are acted upon by unlike forces, the results are unlike. So when like definite aggregations—as the simplest organic cells or the complex organism—are acted upon by unlike forces, the results are unlike, the cells or organisms are differentiated.   But here the changes which arise are definite changes which tend to equilibriate or establish themselves, and also to perpetuate other aggregates of the new variety.   The tendency here, also, is from the less heterogeneous to the more heterogeneous.   Each newly-acquired character is in co-ordination with all the others ; and each more heterogeneous organism tends to the propagation of other organisms similar to itself.

The universal law of balanced action and reaction dominates all aggregates, inorganic and organic alike. No tension could be established otherwise, no two atoms could enter into combination.   Without this balance of forces, a mass or aggregate of any kind would be impossible.

Finally, complex organisms are differentiated to perpetuate—not each one, another entire organism like itself—but dividing the work : one perpetuates the class of elements which may be called the incident forces of the new organism, and the other the opposed or complimentary forces.   Thus, with unlike functions acted upon by unlike conditions, the

sexes become more and more widely, though definitely, differentiated ; each tending always to the
perpetuation of all acquired characters, by transmit-
ting those elements which are the incident forces to
the opposite sex.

The status of each new resulting unit must be
determined by the ability or the inability of the co-
operative elements each to balance the other in their
entirety.   If their mutual adaptations enable them to
do this, the child will combine in modified form
all the qualities of both parents at their best.   This
is Evolution in its highest definite significance.

But *à priori* reasoning on this subject would be
of little value if it cannot be sustained and illustrated by Natural History, past and present.

The distinction between size and structure must
be kept steadily in view.   The immense reptiles of
the past were much less highly organized than our
birds of flight, and much less active in their habits.
It would be impossible to affirm that those sprawling,
sluggish creatures represented a greater aggregate of
organized force than these small incarnated activities,
the barn swallows, or, even than the little restless

humming birds. It would be difficult to make a comparative estimate of the powers of classes so unlike. But the males and females of most species approximate each other in habits and in general structure, as also in size. Here comparison is entirely feasible, and a fair estimate can be made of their relative forces.

The lion is larger, stronger, and handsomer than the lioness ; and he only in most varieties is decorated with a flowing mane. He is far better fitted for his special duty of supplying the family larder, which he does largely for the entire household, it is said, until the young are fully half grown. But the lioness is more complex in structure and in functions than he. His analogue in all respects, though inferior in many, it is she alone who is developed in those organs which have been thought to be of sufficient importance to name the whole class to which they belong, the highest and most important class in the animal kingdom—that of the placental mammals. If she is less strong and valiant in hunting, it may be fairly presumed that her greater heterogeneity is a full equivalent for this deficiency. Then in mental qualities he is the more fervid and more spirited, but she the more constant and more maternal. Her sharpness of intellect has been differently stimulated, but it has not been shown to be inferior to his.

A similar parallel may be instituted between the males and females of every species, and everywhere it will be found that there is a close approximate equivalence of values. This is the more striking because, in the wide range of very unlike beings, the marvellous adaptations of sexual differentiation are extremely varied and the comparison of values must present many curious compensations. But there are some much broader differentiations which distinguish the males and females of many different families of organic beings, animal and vegetable. By attending first to some of these, we may be the better able to estimate the value of more detailed comparisons.

Somewhere within the division Vertebrate runs a dividing line separating the more highly organized animals on the one side, and all the more lowly organized classes, including vegetable life, on the other. On the upper side of this line the males are habitually larger than the females ; on the lower side the law

is reversed—the females are habitually larger than
the males. A fact so broad and well defined as this
must be significant in its bearing upon the equilibrium of the sexes. Moreover, in the division where
the males predominate in size, the females are invariably the more heterogeneous in structure and in functions. In the lower division, the characteristic structure of the females is still sometimes the more heterogeneous, but in a comparatively less degree ; and
there are counteracting conditions to be pointed out
hereafter which obviously must influence their comparative size. With some small quadrupeds, birds,
and reptiles, the size of the two sexes is about the
same ; but it is in the neighborhood of these classes
that our dividing line threads its winding way.

Mr. Darwin is himself the authority for the following statements. Among quadrupeds, when there is
any marked difference in the size of the sexes, the
males are always the larger. This whole division,
therefore, lies either upon or above the line. Birds
also are generally, not always, on the upper side.
Reptiles are grouped more immediately about the
line, above or below. The females of all snakes are

slightly the larger. The rule is reversed with lizards. Some male turtles are the larger, and among frogs, toads, etc., neither sex greatly excels.

Below the line are all fishes ; for no male of any species is known to exceed the female in size. Here also are all invertebrates of every class, a very few insects excepted. The rule holds equally in the sea with its hosts of curious swarming tribes, and, on land, with every variety of crawling, jumping, or flying creatures without jointed backbones. With these I class all hermaphrodites, plants, and all animals which, like plants, establish a community of growth. The ovary always occupies the more central position, and the superior relations to the nutritive processes. Sufficient reasons for this provision are so obvious that they need not be specified ; but so long as an organism is simple, and the whole structure nearly homogeneous, the young, as with higher classes, being directly nourished through maternal intervention, natural selection would inevitably favor the sex which is most important to offspring.

This law would continue up to the point at which *heterogeneity* of *structure and functions* is able to

balance *direct nutrition* in importance as means to
the advancement of the species. At some fixed
point, varying within certain limits, according to the
conditions and habits of the species, there would
arise an equilibrium between these two antagonisms—the direct and the indirect sustenance of offspring. So long as the conditions of life are simple,
nature directly favors the female ; and it is she who
attains the larger growth. But with added complexity
of functions and a higher division of labor, the indirect sustenance of the species, represented by the
raw material of food, and by the greater strength and
activity of muscle and brain to meet the higher conditions of existence, becomes of equal or even of
paramount importance. Here, selecting characters
according to varying conditions of the species, it
becomes useful that the male should attain to the
larger growth and the greater activity.

But this antagonism or opposition of the functions
of sex, though real and continuous, is in reality a
balance of activities—an equilibrium which requires
that at all stages of development there shall be a
virtual equivalence of sex in every species. This is

claimed to be the true meaning of all the curious and varied modifications on either side. *Nature is forced to provide for a balanced expenditure between the sexes of all the greater divisions of force—to maintain not only a differentiated moving equilibrium in each, but also a still wider equilibrium between the two.*

To bring forward evidence in proof of an approximate universal equivalence of the sexes is now directly in point.

In accordance with the uniform plan in all organisms, the pistil in all plants occupies the most protected portion of the flower, the nutritive centre at the point of growth, where the maturing seed can be most directly benefited. The parent plant may be said literally to comprise the two sexes united, as is the rule to a greater or less extent in all compound and bisexual organisms. In every leaf, and in every fragment of the stem, these two polarities are co-operative, while they are separated only in the flower, or rather, only in the double product of the flower. The union of the two elsewhere is shown by the possibility of converting branch and leaf buds into flowers—that is, of separating the united sexualities and their products, to be again reunited in the seed. The same fact is indicated by the double mode of growth and activity upwards and downwards from every axis, by the death of the internode where the equilibrium is destroyed, and by the opposed circulation and balance of functions in leaf and root.

More broadly, there is no organic growth whatever in plant or animal except from an axis or centre —a proof of adapted molecular tensions, more or less complex in their combinations ; and growth consists in adding like tensions in continued maintenance of the organic balance. There is, then, a wide sense in which it may be said that the feminine and the masculine, with their opposed tensions and polarities of forces, are combined in every organism ; but among all higher beings begins from the first *the division of functions* analogous to that which we see in the flower with its separation of stamens and pistils. The entire organism and all modes of activity being, then, necessarily modified diversely in correspondence with one or other of the two phases of the differentiated function, this resulting modification, and this only, whether greater or less in degree

—as in high or low organisms—may be properly called *the difference* arising from sex.   We do not consider that the balanced actions and reactions which work together in the inorganic world are distinctions of sex; that of the two elements in a compound one is masculine and the other feminine.   Nor can we so regard them, for these elements and these forces are continually changing sides, entering into indefinite rearrangements in conjunction with other forces.   Thus what might be distinguished as masculine in one case, would become feminine in the next.

All forces co-operate by successive actions and reactions, and their resulting tensions; but it is only in the organic cell that there arises a definite relation between certain balanced forces.   Every cell is a little organism, like every other of its own type. Therefore, as there must be in every cell a definite set of molecular tensions, and as one half of the molecular forces must be balanced against the other half in maintaining these tensions, it is possible to call the one moiety masculine, and the equivalent one feminine.   But if these names are appropriated to designate this universal organic differentiation, by

what term, then, could we discriminate those differentiations superadded to the other which arise as
unlike modifications resulting from a differentiation
of the reproductive characters ?   It is with these latter that the terms masculine and feminine, with other
related names, are already associated ; and therefore
I shall restrict them to this meaning in the present
paper.

The main plant, then, is of neither sex, properly
speaking, though definite balanced forces co-operate
in every cell of its entire organism.   But when these
balanced forces begin to be differentiated in function
and structure in the two parts of the blossom, in
order that they may each eliminate a special but
unlike product, _. .s differentiation of character is
sex.   The like b : much more complex differentiation in the hig _.r animals—modifying the entire
structure and all its activities—is sex.   The blossom
must be regarded as the first considerable variation
from the ordinary plant system of nutrition ; as the
first division of plant work, which is the work of
simple assimilation of the materials of growth.   This,
let it be remembered, is always balanced or equilib-

riated growth ; and this primary division of the work is assigning to the stamens the duty of elaborating one set of molecular forces, and to the pistils the duty of elaborating a balanced set of molecular forces. The two products united produce the new equilibrium of the parent type.

Division of function, then, is the *origin* of sex. It begins even lower down in the scale of beings than the perfect flower ; but the process in the flower is better known than elsewhere, and is brought up to so clear a differentiation that it is well adapted to be made the type and illustration of the division of function assigned to the sexes universally. The equivalent groups of opposed tensions unite in the embryo, work together, each adding like to like in balanced proportions of growth, and so maintain the organism to the end.

But the *seed* of the flower is as simple in structure as its grandparent the plant. Its first duty is to assimilate food—to grow, to produce root, stem, and leaves asexually—that is, to go on multiplying itself more or less indefinitely without division of work in the uniform nutritive process except in blossoming.

Mr. Spencer argues that there is a direct antagonism between the assimilative process and asexual reproduction. But such an antagonism must be merely superficial. The process is identical. Whether an organism goes on adding like parts to itself, and thus increasing in size, like a higher plant or a compound animal, or whether it continues to add like parts, but sends them adrift to go off independently for themselves—as do all the one-celled and some of the many-celled asexual parents—can be of no characteristic importance. The division or non-division is determined neither by structure nor function, but by unimportant external and internal conditions. If the plant can manufacture woody fibre, the asexual products can cling together to become a large tree; yet the woody fibre at the heart is but dead though undecayed organism. If every like part had been thrown off from the parent from the first, with the same amount of nutriment assimilated, there would be the same amount of growth and life. If the plant cannot manufacture woody fibre, it cannot aggregate a great bulk, in which case it sooner inaugurates the new process of

seeding and colonizing a product equipped to seek
nutriment at a distance.   The low classes of organisms which live in water usually divide often, because
thereby food is better secured.   But on land, and
rooted in the soil, the reverse is true.   The antagonism, then, between a large aggregation of like parts,
and the same number of like parts all separate
or aggregated in small groups, must turn out to be
only a matter of adaptation to unlike conditions, and
not a radical differentiation.   It has been supposed
that separation and reunion of reproductive functions
must necessarily intervene at some stage of growth;
but this is not yet proved, if not already disproved.
The weeping willows mature no seed, yet they are
found thriving everywhere as immense trees ; and
the males, if there are any, of various insects have
never been discovered.

The first rise of a division of functions must be
everywhere accompanied by a corresponding evolution of organs ; yet the formation of differentiated
structure is always expensive and to be avoided
except for some sufficient reason.   The Aphis,
sucking the juices of the plant on which it lives,

must maintain a minute size if it is to make its home
upon a single fragile leaf.   Sexless offspring, sent out
at less cost to the parent, can thrive and multiply
with equal advantage to themselves so long as there
is abundant food and warmth ; but with any disturbance of the equilibrium, provident Nature,
alarmed for the result, begins at once to circumvent
the evil by a division of the reproductive process :
the result is a brood with more perfect endowments,
which can continue the reproduction of the race
either asexually or sexually.   The sea worm,
Octopus, emerging from the egg a neuter individual,
grows to many segments ; then a perfect male or
female forms itself out of one portion of it and
drops off from the neuter parent to continue its life
elsewhere.

The methods are various when the ends to be
attained are the same ; but apparently among all
those beings that have the two modes of propagation,
any disturbance of equilibrium, from whatever cause,
produces an immediate resort to the more expensive
but at the same time the higher and more effective
process of sexual genesis.   Thus a tree may be made

to produce seed by underfeeding or by overfeeding, by various modes of disturbing the roots, or by pruning the branches or merely the leaves, or by slightly girdling the bark. Unsettle the even balance in any way, and, in instant alarm, all the resources of the community are turned to the propagation of a young colony which can be sent off to continue the race elsewhere.

The instinct of the bee teaches it the same lesson. The semi-sexless members of the community can be developed at less cost of nutriment, and their division of work can be performed to advantage if there is a development of no conflicting special instincts ; but with the death of the queen the community is unbalanced, and is in danger of destruction. Some of the young, who would have remained rudimentary in sex to the end but for this unbalance of functions in the body politic, are immediately nurtured into complete young queens—a process readily accomplished by giving them more in quantity and more stimulating diet, and a royal cell in which there is room enough to allow of the necessary growth and development. No one can fail to see the analogy between this process and that of developing a leaf bud into a flower. The annual autumn destruction of the now useless drones is but a curious modification of similar vegetable economy seen in the annual fall of the leaf.

Fanciful as the suggestion may seem to many persons, I am disposed to regard the mother spider of some species as a little modification of the community-system in her own person. She aggregates to herself in bulk similar elements to those which the aphides would have thrown off in sexless individuals, then uses this acquired energy for the benefit of her higher grade of offspring. The habit of spinning a web and lying in wait for food enables her to thrive to best advantage single-handed ; and her comparatively larger size is itself a benefit, enabling her to attack larger prey and to support a numerous progeny. The very small male spider, active and self-supporting, may be regarded as the more advanced analogue of the stamens of a flower,—while the female is at once the representative of the pistil and of the entire plant combined. True to a similar economy of instinct, she comprehends that the best method in which her partner can further serve the interests of their offspring, is to suffer himself to be eaten up for their sustenance.

If, among some of the low orders of beings, there is any more satisfactory method of explaining the exceeding disparity of the sexes in bulk or the aggregation of forces, and in corresponding duties, I cannot find it. The larger here is always the mother, and she bears the whole burden of nurturing the offspring. A cirriped, less fully developed than the spider, will illustrate an intermediate reproductive type between that and a polyp or a plant. The male of the cirriped, without a mouth or nutritive organs, is a mere parasite upon the female or the hermaphrodite, and is but a mere speck in comparison with the larger organism. One must regard these and similar remarkable expedients, adapted always to the special exigencies of habits and surroundings, as results effected through natural selection in the common interest of the race—selection limited by the necessity of maintaining an equilibriated activity under all organic conditions.

Mr. Spencer designates a "stable equilibrium" as

that in which "any excess of one of the forces at work, itself generates, by the deviation it produces, certain counter forces that eventually outbalance it, and initiate an opposite deviation." This is an admirable statement of my idea of the balanced relations of the opposite sexes. In every type of beings the sexes are necessarily in " stable equilibrium." Thus, in the flower of a plant, as the pistil is in the central, best nourished, and most protected position, the stamens are usually many more in number, even when the pistil is compound or several in a group. An ouale has gathered about the germ an expensive supply of nutriment ; but, on the other hand, the pollen grains are a multitude, most of which are wasted of necessity. We may regard this simply as an extra provision for insuring the fructification of the seed ; but there is also some ground for supposing that it is a mode of expending equal amounts of the unlike forces, in maintenance of the necessary equilibrium ; for when the two sexes are borne upon separate plants, the amount of pollen is enormously increased, while on the companion tree the flower is more or less shorn of all superfluous parts, and is sometimes reduced, as in the cones, to a simple naked scale.

Comparisons can be also made among the higher types where sex and individuality are both complete and associated. And yet here the equation must be much less direct and simple. As both sexes become more complex in structure and functions, and also more characteristically unlike in proportion, one class of activities must be often balanced by some very different class. Thus greater complexity of structure may be offset by greater bulk and strength, or by any excess of activity in one or in several directions. From the conservation of force, the convertibility of like modes of force, a perpetual readjustment is essential. The many possible combinations, varying with unlike conditions, often render the equation extremely difficult of statement. Of course it can be only approximate as applied to individuals ; but in a species, or in a large number of averages, it may be literally accurate. I have drawn up the following table of comparative equations : the *mean* of characters in each class being taken as zero.

Tabular View of Equations in Organic Nature.

———

The Asexual Plane.

A given amount of growth anywhere } = { The same amount of growth everywhere.

Whether the result be large or small aggregates, the equation remains unchanged.

The Sexual Plane.

Males. | Females.

PLANTS.

Stamens and their Pro-ducts } = { Pistils and their Products.

INSECTS.

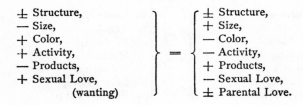

Males	Females
± Structure,	± Structure,
— Size,	+ Size,
+ Color,	— Color,
+ Activity,	— Activity,
— Products,	+ Products,
+ Sexual Love,	— Sexual Love,
(wanting)	± Parental Love.

FISHES.

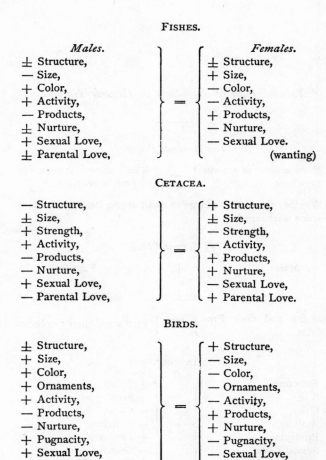

Males.		*Females.*
± Structure,		± Structure,
— Size,		+ Size,
+ Color,		— Color,
+ Activity,	=	— Activity,
— Products,		+ Products,
± Nurture,		— Nurture,
+ Sexual Love,		— Sexual Love.
± Parental Love,		(wanting)

CETACEA.

— Structure,		+ Structure,
± Size,		± Size,
+ Strength,		— Strength,
+ Activity,	=	— Activity,
— Products,		+ Products,
— Nurture,		+ Nurture,
+ Sexual Love,		— Sexual Love,
— Parental Love,		+ Parental Love.

BIRDS.

± Structure,		+ Structure,
+ Size,		— Size,
+ Color,		— Color,
+ Ornaments,		— Ornaments,
+ Activity,	=	— Activity,
— Products,		+ Products,
— Nurture,		+ Nurture,
+ Pugnacity,		— Pugnacity,
+ Sexual Love,		— Sexual Love,
— Parental Love,		+ Parental Love.

HERBIVORA.

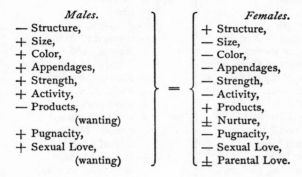

Males.		*Females.*
— Structure,		+ Structure,
+ Size,		— Size,
+ Color,		— Color,
+ Appendages,		— Appendages,
+ Strength,	=	— Strength,
+ Activity,		— Activity,
— Products,		+ Products,
(wanting)		± Nurture,
+ Pugnacity,		— Pugnacity,
+ Sexual Love,		— Sexual Love,
(wanting)		± Parental Love.

CARNIVORA.

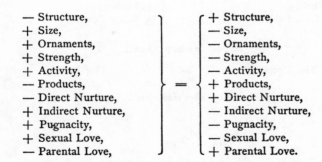

— Structure,		+ Structure,
+ Size,		— Size,
+ Ornaments,		— Ornaments,
+ Strength,		— Strength,
+ Activity,		— Activity,
— Products,	=	+ Products,
— Direct Nurture,		+ Direct Nurture,
+ Indirect Nurture,		— Indirect Nurture,
+ Pugnacity,		— Pugnacity,
+ Sexual Love,		— Sexual Love,
— Parental Love,		+ Parental Love.

MAN.

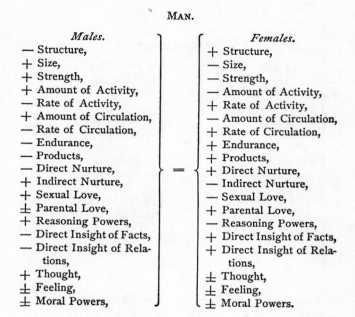

Males.		*Females.*
— Structure,		+ Structure,
+ Size,		— Size,
+ Strength,		— Strength,
+ Amount of Activity,		— Amount of Activity,
— Rate of Activity,		+ Rate of Activity,
+ Amount of Circulation,		— Amount of Circulation,
— Rate of Circulation,		+ Rate of Circulation,
— Endurance,		+ Endurance,
— Products,		+ Products,
— Direct Nurture,	=	+ Direct Nurture,
+ Indirect Nurture,		— Indirect Nurture,
+ Sexual Love,		— Sexual Love,
± Parental Love,		+ Parental Love,
+ Reasoning Powers,		— Reasoning Powers,
— Direct Insight of Facts,		+ Direct Insight of Facts,
— Direct Insight of Relations,		+ Direct Insight of Relations,
+ Thought,		± Thought,
± Feeling,		± Feeling,
± Moral Powers,		± Moral Powers.

Result in every Species.

The Females   =   The Males.

Comprehensive Result.

Sex   =   Sex.

Or,

Organic Equilibrium in Physiological and Psychological Equivalence of the Sexes.

These approximate equations are largely collated from Mr. Darwin's extended comparisons of secondary sexual characters. Fixing attention, as he does, upon masculine characters only, there seems to be no equilibrium of sex ; but, holding the feminine characters up beside the others in a balanced view, the equilibrium is restored. The two leading philosophers of Evolution, each after his own method of investigation, being intent upon explaining the wider equilibrium between organic nature and its external conditions, it becomes fairly credible that they may have failed to give satisfactory attention to the lesser equilibria of sex, of each individual organism, and of every organic cell. If these are not each moving points of simpler adjustments within wider and wider systems of more complex adjustments, then I fail utterly to comprehend the first principle of organization.

So long as nutrition remains the most important organic function, the best-nurtured individuals might be expected to develop females ; and observation confirms this expectation. But as an offset to this advantageous tendency, the males of most insects are

earliest developed ; and we may infer from this and
other facts that they have a correspondingly quicker,
though feebler, general circulation. As a rule, they
certainly possess greater, often much greater, activity, and greater brilliancy of color. Insects are
an immense and most varied class, yet these main
differences, variously modified, are almost universal.
When the sexes acquire unlike habits, as sometimes
happens, it is the females that attain the best nutritive conditions ; but it is the males that gain or retain the highest locomotive powers. Some female
insects, as certain flies, are blood-suckers, while the
males sip only the juices of plants. Some other
males, in their final stage of development, have no
mouths, and live only a brief life, though the females
eat and live till their eggs are deposited, but then die
also. Conversely, many females of moths, grasshop-
pers, glowworms, etc., have no wings. Others, which
are parasitic, in their last development lose locomotive organs which belonged to an earlier stage of
growth, though the males still retain these.

But greater activity in one sex may fairly balance
superior nutritive functions in the other ; while, by the

law of inheritance, their posterity will be equally
advantaged by both, and lifted towards a higher development in both lines of evolution, converging in
themselves.

Turning to psychical traits, if all those instincts
tending to the propagation of the race, on which Mr.
Darwin has laid such stress in " Sexual Selection," are
most active in the male line, there are corresponding
traits in nearly all females, equally important and of
equal significance in mental evolution. All insect
mothers act with the utmost wisdom and good faith,
and with a beautiful instinctive love towards a posterity which they are directly never to caress or nurture,
as mothers do who are higher up in the scale of
being. These tiny creatures work with the skill of
carpenters and masons, and often with a prudence
and forethought which is even more than human ; for
they never suffer personal ease or advantage to prevent their making proper provision for their young.
Some of them merely deposit their eggs where there
will be abundant nourishment for the larva ; others
search for the proper food—perhaps the young of other
creatures—and seal them up together in nests, or by

similar marvellous devices promote the survival of their race.

That all Evolution has been carried forward by small successive stages, can hardly be doubted by many persons who will devote the necessary attention to the accumulative evidence on this point. But that all this has been accomplished *without intelligent plan or prevision*, certainly is not a theory essential to the hypothesis of Evolution. On the contrary, that Nature, as we know it, could have originated otherwise than through the natural creation or adaptation of a *co-operative constitution* of things, co-ordinating all substances, sentient and unsentient, is, to my apprehension, utterly incredible. Nowhere is there higher evidence of Design, and of the existence of a true sentient force co-operative in every organism, than in the wondrous instincts of insect life.

But, be this as it may—for these subjects are not now under discussion—all the accessories, physical and psychical, which accompany female instincts in the invertebrates (parental love) must be considered as fairly equal to correlative male instincts (sexual love). The one impels to the initiation, the other to the

preservation, of offspring ; the one leads to vivid,
concentrated impulses ; the other to calmer, self-
forgetting, steady affection : both united, to the
higher and higher development of the race. We
need only compare one such picture of instinctive
parental love, as that drawn by Professor Agassiz, of
the common horse-hair worm, sewing herself like a
living threaded needle again and again through the
mass of eggs she was trying to protect, when they
were successively broken up and taken from her, with
Mr. Darwin's repeated citations of courtship, as a
strong phase of Evolution. We shall comprehend
that the more placid love of offspring is an equivalent
equally needed in combination in all higher development, male and female ; and everywhere accompanied
with at least as much intelligence in its manifestations. The great majority of the "homes without
hands," among the highest evidences that we have of
animal intelligence, as expended in their construction,
are in whole or in part the work of females. The
undeveloped female constructs the cell of the bee, and
probably of all kindred species ; and birds work together in nest-building, the little mother generally

taking upon herself the larger share of duty. It requires a great amount of male surplus activity, to be
expended physically in motion and psychically in
emotion, as well as a good deal of extra ornamentation
and brilliancy of coloring, to balance the extra direct
and indirect nurture, the love, and the ingenuity
which the mother birds, and even the insects, bestow
upon their young.

Fervor of feeling undoubtedly has something to
do with brilliancy of coloring. This is shown in the
nuptial plumage of many birds, and in the vivid
colors, more or less temporary, in higher animals.
Dark-colored and bright-colored individuals in all
species, man included, are of a more excitable temperament than the light-colored individuals ; and,
carefully comparing whole varieties of the dark
and light-colored in the same species, the rule is
equally universal. The African and the pure Cau-
casian are, perhaps, the two extremes as to fervor
of temperament among human beings ; but where
the complexity of characters is so great, as among
mankind, a direct comparison in these respects is
often impossible ; yet, in a general way, other things

equal, the rule holds beyond a question. Moreover, upon the principle of the due balance and division of the functions in the higher stages of evolution, in the human race, fervor of feeling, or *quickness of general sensibility*, must be regarded rather as a feminine than as a masculine character. As Mr. Darwin has pointed out, women are rather brighter-colored than men, though there is no considerable difference in this respect, as between one sex and the other. Nor should there be any in sustenance of our theory ; since against the wider or higher sensibility of the female, must be placed sexual fervor, which, through all evolution has remained characteristically male. On this plane, therefore, comparisons must be made when treating of the relations of color, not between the sexes, but between the lighter and darker races and individuals.

Below man, more especially in the herbivora, in birds and in insects, fervor of feeling and brightness of color are in such direct relations that they everywhere rise and fall together. The males are greatly the superiors in the psychical and the physical expressions of the same related fact. Individuals differ from each other in each sex. I cannot offer direct data to prove that the more vigorous and excitable bird or quadruped, in the same sex, is also the more brilliantly colored ; but I appeal to the direct observation of every reader to sustain me in the assertion that, other things equal, this is a universal law. We see it in all our domestic animals. The most active and thriving are sure to be the brightest, the most symmetrical. Such a result would arise, also, from *indirect* causation ; for, all acquirements being *transmitted* equally to offspring of both sexes, in the females, the distinctive masculine character of brighter coloring would of course tend to develop most readily and fully in the more vigorous. The facts sustain the theory.

It has been supposed that color in the petals and other parts of a flower is directly related to the degree of heat evolved during the flowering process. It is entirely certain that color, under all circumstances, is directly related to rates and amounts of motion under the forms of light and heat, more especially the former. But in organized life, motion and emotion are but two phases of the same process,

or at least are something closely akin to this in relation.

Then is sexual selection more needed in accounting for the brilliant plumage of birds, than for the
color of the red blood in their veins, or for the bright
yellow and pure white of their eggs, and the characteristic brilliant mottling of many egg-shells ? If
this form of selection could not have operated in
producing the almost matchless tintings and orderly
harmonies of color in various sea-shells, or in flowers
and fruits, then why insist upon its activity in butterflies, birds, quadrupeds ? They have a sense of color,
doubtless, but they evince a higher sense of complemental attractions, dependent upon influences much
more fundamental than color—a fact which Mr. Darwin has abundantly recognized. With similar influences we are all familiar in human experience ; for
beauty and strength, however attractive, when weighed
in the balance with other qualities, are often found
wanting.

We know that all the darker-colored fruits have
more flavor of the special kind peculiar to them than
the light-colored varieties. Take the light and dark

cherries ; the white, red, and black currants ; the yellow, red, and black raspberries, or any other of the earth's numerous berries and larger fruits in illustration. I think it will be found, also, that the highly-colored fruit-bearers are the most vigorous and hardy growers; and that color is largely related to vigor of condition, and to general activity of functions ; and hence, that the males of all beings, as less directly related to the nutrition of the young, can better afford to become brightly colored ; can better afford to entail this added quality upon their offspring, to the greater beautifying of the world.

On the principle of the equivalence of the sexes, superior brightness of color should be a true masculine character among all the lower classes of beings.

We are prepared, then, to return again to the insects with a better comprehension of the part which color is supposed to take in the balance of their sexual characters. The superior nutritive functions, the advantages of a larger size in maturing many eggs, and the active pre-maternal instincts in the females, are regarded as equitably balanced by superior activity of muscle and greater sexual fervor, with its close relation to brilliancy of color. Each heritage, transmitted, promotes evolution.

We turn from insects—many of them, in their later development, little centres of perpetual motion which consumes an immense amount of force—to fishes, their antipodes in this respect. As a class, fishes are also extremely active and rapid in their movements: but it is an activity in part counter-balanced by the density of the fluid in which they live, and therefore resulting in much less expenditure of force. Also they are cold-blooded, expending little for vital warmth; and though the larger majority of species are carnivorous, yet, living in regions where their food also abounds, they are more nearly in conditions resembling those of the terrestrial herbivores than the carnivores. Chiefly, they seize and swallow prey weaker than themselves. I cannot learn that any fish, male or female, is known to hunt or forage for another; but every individual, young and old, after it ceases to depend upon the supply of nutriment laid up for it in the egg, is compelled to obtain food for itself.

The entire class has but small development of

brain and of the special senses.   Judging from their
nervous system, they are dull of hearing, have very
little of the sense of taste, but something more of
smell, and still more of sight—the latter essential to
them in obtaining food.   The females live simply to
find and appropriate food, to grow, and to produce
an almost incredible multitude of eggs.   Their whole
stock of energy is wellnigh consumed in these directions, leaving no surplus for higher development. They
manifest but little attraction towards the opposite
sex, and still less affection for their own young.   In
size they invariably exceed the males—sometimes are
even many times larger—often with no scruples
against devouring their own species or their own
offspring.

How, then, does Nature maintain a balance between these voracious female *consumers and repro-
ducers* and the smaller males?   When the disparity
in size is great, by selecting several males to one
female.   Polyandry is practised accordingly.   It is
a higher version of the relations of stamens and
pistils.   If we suppose, as with insects, that the best-
nurtured ova become female, natural selection can

regulate the proportions in every brood so as to maintain the equilibrium.

The sexes approach each other in size among some higher fishes, and though the numerical data are very insufficient, yet such evidence as we have leads to the conclusion that they also become more nearly equal in numbers. Then all male fishes approximate the other sex in the amount of reproductive products much more closely than any other class of animals. Still, there is a large margin not yet balanced (unless it be done numerically). How, then, do male fishes utilize surplus force? Their respiratory system is relatively larger, showing their greater activity; they quarrel more as rivals, they are more brilliantly colored; a few have marked secondary characters; and in many widely different orders the *parental instinct* is very fairly developed *in the males*, though the least trace of maternal instinct in the females is rare and exceptional.

To the necessity of maintaining the equivalence of the sexes, add progress and advantage to the species. It seems inevitable that all piscine evolution, physical and psychical, aside from mere homogeneous increase in size, should be carried forward in the male line. With many carnivorous species in the same localities, all preying upon each other, each must continue to be extremely prolific or risk complete extinction. The female, as most directly related to nutrition, must of necessity be absorbed in this direction. On land there can be no such close and continuous competition. All the conditions vary more widely, and hence the various species have become much more differentiated. Vegetable and animal life are more directly balanced on land than in salt or fresh water ; hence more land animals become vegetarians. Plants directly, and animals both directly and indirectly, are more dependent upon the atmosphere, as air-breathing, than when breathing through a water medium ; and the habits of different land races become so widely unlike that there is less continuous close rivalry between a large number of nearly-allied beings. It is a more remote rivalry, or confined to a fewer number of similarly constituted antagonists.

There are more aids towards a continuous wider division of duties among terrestrial animals—not

merely as between species and species, but between
sex and sex in the same species, and function and
function in the same individual. Evolution, therefore, can be promoted through the males and females
alike, and perhaps even to an equal degree, among
the higher orders of beings.

Yet there is advance, even among fishes, physiologically and psychologically. The higher classes
approach the mammalia in structure much more
nearly than the lower. " Certain fishes, belonging to
several families, make nests, and some of these fishes
take care of their young when hatched. Both sexes
of the brightly-colored *Crenilabrus, massa,* and *melops,*
work together in building their nests with sea-weed,
shells, etc. But the males of certain fishes do all the
work, and afterwards take exclusive care of the
young." " The males of certain other fishes inhabiting
South America and Ceylon, and belonging to two
distinct orders, have the extraordinary habit of hatching the eggs laid by the females within their mouths or
bronchial cavities." The paternal nurses sometimes,
like the Promotis, sit upon the eggs, and others are
represented as "continually employed in gently leading

back the young to the nest when they stray too far."
With fishes, the love and care of the young are
recognized as specially male duties. The cuiious
sea-horses (*Hippocampi*) and the Pipe fishes faithfully
carry the young about everywhere in their pouches.
These duties are usually accompanied by brilliancy
of color more than at other seasons, and their bright
hues are much superior to the colors of the females.
Referring to the genus *Solenostoma*, in which "the
female is much more vividly colored and spotted than
the male, and she alone has a marsupial sack and
hatches the eggs ;" Mr. Darwin says : "It is improbable that this *remarkable double inversion of
character* in the female should be an accidental coincidence." He distinctly recognizes the close relation between the accompanying emotional states,
which must lead to the performance of these higher
duties, and superior brilliancy of coloring. Parental
instincts are also assigned to the male.

Now, if female fishes were not, by structure and
surrounding conditions, narrowly limited to the two
functions, growth and reproduction, with only so
much physical and psychical development as will best

promote these ends, the transmitted love of offspring would be oftener developed. The race could thus advance rapidly to a higher plane. But so long as multitudes of ova are indispensable to race-preservation, and a large maternal organism the needful accompaniment, these two characters must take precedence of higher development.

The conditions are not greatly more favorable to evolution in sea-life than in plant-life. Plants still alternate between the lower and higher methods of reproduction, and have neither gained nor can expend energy through locomotion. Fishes, much higher in structure and functions, tend slowly upwards under disadvantages—the males, by a fair division of duties, leading the way in all psychological and functional development.

Then why, since "the law of the equal transmission of characters to both sexes" cannot "commonly prevail" among fishes — for all higher mental characters must at best be very slowly developed in these poor "functional mothers"—why is it not probable that the piscine males will in time "become *as superior in mental endowments* to the females as the

peacock is in ornamental plumage to the peahen?"*
Influences are at work to prevent, or greatly retard,
the development of the sex closely related to nutrition, as are all female fishes. But male fishes are less
heavily taxed for offspring, are able to remain of
smaller size with no disadvantage to themselves and
little to the race, and are so circumstanced that it is
not easy to expend excessive force in physical
activity. Why should they not already have advanced wonderfully, *in comparison with their females,
in brain development and mental evolution?* If a
greater supply of oxygen was requisite, they could
even have acquired lungs, as whales have done. That
almost no progress has been made in this direction
by any one of the many species, is significant. It
would be difficult to assign any reason why the male
development has remained about as stationary as the
female, except that of the necessity for a steady
moving equilibrium between the sexes—for a detailed
adaptation and complemental balance in the reproductive elements in every new individual. The race
would thus be averaged in endowments, held upon the

* "Descent of Man," Vol. II., p. 313.

same essential level, and destined only to rise slowly together. That the higher males are habitually the most active, as well as the most ardent, and that it is they who have generally developed the parental instincts, is explained and made easy of comprehension.

Reptiles, closely allied to fishes in temperament and somewhat in habits, yet rather higher in struc ture, and living wholly or in part on land, have taken just those relative characters which are required to maintain sex equilibrium in the different species. The females are much less prolific than fishes; the males are the more active and the brighter colored usually; and the sexes are about equal in size. As a rule, neither parent expends much energy in the nurture of the young; yet there are exceptions in which the care of offspring seems to be divided about equally between the sexes. The female of the Surinam toad carries the eggs about on her back (where they are placed by the male) for about eighty days, till they become perfect frogs. The toad, *Bufo obstetricans*, binds the chaplets of eggs about his own thighs, carrying them around till the eyes of the young are formed, when he deposits them in the water to become tadpoles. The gelatinous mass in which the young are placed is known to contain nutriment. Mr. Darwin finds it "surprising that frogs and toads should not have acquired more strongly-marked sexual differences;" but on the theory of the balance of functions the surprise vanishes. They are equal in size, and the extra fervor of temperament, with slight structural modifications, should balance the greater reproductive tax. The males have also a higher development of vocal organs.

With other reptiles the young are produced alive. We find a variously modified balance of characters; but it appears that the males always exceed the females in activity of habits—the one sex moving about actively while the other lies basking in the sun —or in size, requiring more energy both to build up, sustain, and move the larger organism; or in vivid coloring, and in many curious modifications of structure. These external signs of expended force are equal, we may suppose, in each case to the surplus feminine force devoted to offspring. Lizards have strongly-marked secondary characters.

The warm-blooded Cetaceans—whales, porpoises, dolphins, etc.—though living in the sea, like fishes, breathe through lungs like land animals ; with wonderful adaptations of structure to their modes of life. These have comparatively large, active brains, and are well advanced physiologically and psychologically. But the females have progressed equally with the males, and have inherited the traditional feminine characters, with adapted complex organisms, though it seems to be almost certain that, as with other sea animals, parental love must have been originally first developed in the males.

It was proved impossible to leave the mothers behind in evolution ; impossible to divert functions of direct nutrition from their normal development ! And parental love must precede nurture. In place of the multitudes of spawn left to chance for development, as with fishes, their few young ones are nursed with maternal care, and even with the instincts of intense and self-sacrificing affection.

" The female Dugong produces generally only one young at a birth, and to this the mother bears such strong affection that, if the young is speared, the mother will not depart, but is sure to be taken also. The Malays consider this animal as almost typical of maternal affection. The young utter a short and sharp cry, and are said to shed tears, which are carefully preserved by the common people as a charm, under the notion that they will secure the affections of those whom they love, as they attract the mother to the young Dugong." *   This devoted mother, in popular language still called a fish—the form fish-like, but the structure that of a mammal, with related psychological characters—is immensely higher in the scale of being than the little Stickleback, who can devour her own offspring with excellent appetite.   But the male Stickleback—a nest-builder and a solicitous, careful nurse to the tender young—has these higher functions assigned to him, on our theory, as a balance to the absorbing nutritive tax demanded of the prolific female.   What characters, then, have been selected in the male Dugong and other sea mammals in maintenance of the desired equilibrium?

Professor Owen finds that with the Dugongs, as with the Narwhals, "the permanent tusks of the

* "English Cyclopædia."

female are arrested in their growth and remain throughout life concealed within the substance of the bones and integuments." He has discovered other sexual differences in dentition, apparently of much significance. As with the horns of land herbivora, they are "extra male appendages." Whether once possessed and now lost by the females, or whether originally acquired by the males, but not developed in the females, this difference may be assigned to unlike nutritive functions; the females having but little force to expend in tusk-growing. The many differences which may probably exist between the habits of the sexes in the sea tribes, with whose lives man has but little acquaintance, must remain largely unknown to us. That, in addition to structural modifications, the males have acquired the usual male characters of the higher animals, there is every reason to suppose.

Porpoises roll, tumble, leap from the water. On a clear day the sailors on the mast-head can see the Sperm Whale leaping into the air so high that he can be observed "at a distance of six miles;" he can swim ten or twelve miles an hour. The whole whale group swim rapidly, plunge, leap, and expend much energy in their uncouth sea sports. It is physiologically certain that the males must be the more active. With the Sperm Whales it is admitted that they are also the larger, but among most of the species both sexes seem to go on growing almost indefinitely ; though the males of the same ages are probably of greater bulk than the females. Dolphins and Porpoises, not attaining to the great size of the others, have relatively even larger brains. Brain consumes force and guarantees psychical development. Their intelligence is supposed to equal that of any quadruped, and it seems to be distributed between the sexes in a similar manner, the male characters being much like those of the land herbivora.

All the species are highly social, often travelling together in shoals. The Manitees put their young in the centre of the tribe, to protect them from enemies.

They and the Dugongs hold their young with the pectoral fins almost as a woman might take her child in her arms. Some whales are found in pairs, the mothers closely followed by their young, for whom they are ready to sacrifice life itself ; so that to harpoon the young one is to secure the mother, who refuses to forsake it, and is easily captured.

How unlike is all this to the habits of fishes, whose females, as a rule, seem to have absolutely no love of offspring, and often almost no social instincts! But then how is any mother to love a thousand or a million children in a single brood? The race must attain to superior conditions, in which it is able to propagate itself through the longer life of a few individuals, before it can be expected to rise much in psychical development ; and neither the males nor the females will make any considerable amount of progress unless the other sex can be advanced also in the same proportion. In general structure, the sexes in all grades of being have always continued to be nearly identical.

With the important rise in division of functions implied in warm blood and active habits, associated with higher structure, nutrition becomes more or less subordinate to many activities, physical and psychical. Locomotion, sensations, emotions, instincts, intelligence, all adapt themselves to special higher uses and modes of living.

Mr. Spencer has shown that, on mechanical principles, every increase in size requires more than an equal increase of strength to balance the activities. Hence we find that among all higher animals it is the rule that the males shall expend the most energy in growth and locomotion, and shall be the active outside partners in every family firm. The females devote a corresponding larger share of direct force to social obligations, as more nutrition and care to the young, more skill, time, affection, and intellect to all direct family necessities.

Most male birds assist more or less in nest-building, and in brooding and feeding the dependent household. All these are force-exhausting duties ; so is the duty of family defence, of enlivening song, and perpetual cheerful activity. Dr. Carpenter says : " In general, it is to be remarked that the attention which the young receive after they break the shell is prolonged in proportion as the plumage, and especially the feathers of flight, are to be of a more perfect character ; so that, in this comparatively trifling variation, we have an illustration of the general law that the higher the grade of development which

the being is ultimately to attain, the more is it assisted in the early stages by its parent." Now, let us
apply this statement to some of the most ornamental
birds, such as Birds of Paradise and many of the
gallinaceous birds. All these require prolonged nurture ; and yet it is among exactly these classes that
the males are polygamous, or at least are very indif-
ferent providers, who devolve the entire care of the
young upon the females. It would be expected, then,
that the latter should remain, as they do, simple and
unornamented, while the surplus male energy is converted into magnificent plumage.

Conversely, among a few species of birds in several orders, the males take upon themselves the duties
of incubation and the feeding of the young, and, as it
should be upon our hypothesis, the sexes in these
cases effect a complete exchange of many characters.
In an Australian species of the Turnix, the females.
are nearly twice as large as the males. In an Indian
species the male " wants the black on the throat and
neck, and the whole tone of the plumage is lighter
and less pronounced than that of the female." The
females are " more vociferous, more pugnacious ; " and

it is they, and not the males, who are kept like game-cocks for fighting.   After laying their eggs, the females "associate in flocks, and leave the males to sit on them."   The male of the cassowary also does maternal duty, and he "would be thought by any one to be the female, from his smaller size and from the appendages and naked skin about his head being less brightly colored."

Mr. Wallace, who first called attention to the relation between less bright colors and nursing duties, considers it "a crucial test that obscure colors have been acquired for the sake of protection during the nesting period."   Mr. Darwin regards it as a reversed case of sexual selection, "steadily adding to the attractions of the females."   Certain it is, "an almost complete transposition of the instincts, habits, disposition, color, size, and of some points of structure, has been effected between the two sexes."   It is noteworthy that these opposed groups of masculine and feminine characters *may be regarded as true equivalents ;* that the protective love for offspring, with the devotion of energy which it instigates, is equal to a large amount of superior beauty, activity, and chivalry.

Some similar averaging of physiological and affectional qualities in birds seems to obtain invariably—always grouped in more or less marked contrast. The cow birds and cuckoos of both sexes, escape nursing duties by depositing their eggs in the nests of other birds, yet the males of both are brighter in color than the females, and the male cuckoos at least are larger in size. But the females provide the early supply of nutrition in the egg-shell, and in them is developed the instinct to search for and find the appropriate nests in which the young ones can be properly hatched. The restless anxiety which these gipsey mothers manifest when a nest is to be stolen, so unlike the assured movements of the little housekeeper in her own home, is yet evidence of a psychological development unlike that of the males. When we consider that the general habits of these parasitic birds are alike in both sexes, all their unlike characters must be regarded as fairly balanced.

The occasional nutritive tax must be less influential in producing differences than any wide diversity in the habits of the two sexes. The large majority of birds best known to us have nearly the same modes of life. They live largely under very similar conditions, share their housekeeping cares, and migrate together or at nearly the same time. The result is that the male is usually rather larger, brighter, and a better singer : he is always more or less superior in activity, yet the sexes strongly resemble each other. The males have few marked special modifications, and generally none at all.

Whenever the more brilliant sex, in addition, is "ornamented by all sorts of combs, wattles, protuberances, horns, air-distended sacs, topknots, naked shafts, plumes, and lengthened feathers gracefully springing from all parts of the body," it appears that there is invariably some conspicuous difference in their habitual methods of life. Our domestic fowls live in the midst of abundant and easily obtained food. The hens produce many and large eggs, give the warmth of their bodies to hatch the chickens, and lead the young about for weeks together, often watching patiently to see them eat while they themselves fast. The cocks feed themselves abundantly, strut idly up and down the walks, fight their rivals, bully the hens, crow vigorously, and can afford to wear spurs and an abundance of other ornaments, as an easy method of utilizing the surplus nutriment which is not needed in developing the structure, or in further increasing the size of the species. The males of wild turkeys associate in groups of from ten to a hundred, living a merry life, much of the time by themselves, and killing the young ones by beating them on the head when they meet ; while the mothers, with their children, by the single family, or in larger parties, follow on behind, at a safe distance, gleaning the scantier fare, but ever ready with protective maternal instincts.

Mr. Darwin is confident there is some close relation between polygamy and all clases of extra male appendages. There is some close relation, also, between polygamy and easily accessible food—food of the kind which must be obtained by each individual, young and old, chiefly for itself. Mr. Darwin does not know that the lower species are ever polygamous ; and the South African lion, the only large flesheater known to be polygamous, is the only one, also, " in the whole group of the terrestrial carnivora, that

presents well-marked sexual characters." Polygamy
means evading the equitable share of parental duties by
birds or beasts, and with land animals is feasible only
among such as find food on the ground or in easily
accessible locations, so that the mothers can assume
the whole protective burden in rearing the offspring.

But whenever, for any cause, as with a very large
number of the herbivora, the males lead different
lives from the females and are freed from family care,
they are found also to have varied to a greater or less
extent from other males to which they are allied in
structure, and still more from the females of their
own species. Whether these males are or are not
polygamous may be non-essential, provided they acquire different habits and share unequal or unlike
duties. Many of the herbivora wander about in
groups, the sexes generally separated, but the females
and the young sometimes accompanied by a few
males of large size and warlike habits. Thus the
sexes of the reindeer separate in winter, meeting
again at their common places of resort in spring—a
custom of mutual advantage to all parties.

These grazing mothers, by the habits of separa-

tion, are often saved from the turbulence of quarrelsome neighbors, from rapid marches, or from distant
migrations, and are benefited by a larger supply of
food at periods when they have little surplus energy
to waste, or when the tender young might be destroyed by toilsome journeys. The less burdened
males, with abundant surplus energy seeking utilization, become yet stronger, larger, more vigorous, by
their additional exertion. Their offspring profit by
this added vigor as essentially as by the extra
maternal care. The young of carnivora and of birds
are no more really benefited by the food which
is procured and brought to them by their male
parents.

It would not be an advantage to any of the higher
races that the sexes should very greatly differ in size.
This inequality would tend perpetually to correct itself.
Yet there must be a limit to the inheritance of the
larger bulk by the females, whose strength and vigor
are demanded in other directions. Hence the extra
male appendages, the great horns which often grow
to enormous size and yet fall off every year ; the long
and brilliant feathers of the peacock, the argus pheas-

ant, the birds of paradise ; the redundant masculine appendages of so many different species ; most, if not all of them, pertain only to such organisms as are exonerated from the burden of domestic duties by the nature of the food upon which they subsist.

It seems to be inevitable that these variations should be classed as secondary sexual characters and intimately associated with reproduction. The fundamental social instincts, tending to the genesis or to the preservation of offspring, have generally received their highest development, not both together in the same sex, but one in either sex. But the males of the herbivores and the gallinaceous birds manifest almost no parental love. Their entire psychical development, at least in all its social phases, is apparently gained through the sexual instincts, with their reactions, as manifested in rivalry with its whole range of warlike impulses, its craft, its vanities and sexual courtesies. The peacock can afford the time and develop the talents for displaying his fine plumage on all occasions ; while the busy little householder, who studies how to weave the best straw into his domicile in the best manner possible, who sits duti-

fully upon the nest now and then, or brings the break-
fast to his more patient spouse, who rejoices as she
does over the new-born chicks, and does his best to
feed them and to give them flying lessons when they
are old enough—this more highly-developed and bet-
ter-balanced personage has neither time nor energy
to devote to the mere graces of life. He may sing
very little, may be scarcely larger or brighter-colored
than his mate, and not greatly more warlike or chival-
rous ; yet who shall say that his gifts are not fairly
equivalent to those of his more showy cousins, the
Gallinaciæ ?

It is a simple question of the conservation of
force. The beings of allied species, male and female,
must be supposed to have reached a similar plane of
development, physiological and psychological, and to
have acquired the use and partial control of about
the same amounts of energy. Used in one direction,
it cannot be applied to another. Mental activity
consumes force as certainly as does motion or any
other mode of energy, and thoughts or feelings
developed in one channel imply limitations in some
other.

Where female offspring inherit what may properly be considered as male characters, they belong generally to an active, vigorous race, and the males will be found often to have inherited in turn from the females. The reindeer is the only species in which the females have horns nearly as large as the males; but they belong to an extremely hardy and active tribe, which, when tamed, are able to draw sledges with great speed and endurance. The young, after a few days, are strong enough to follow the mother everywhere, and soon become comparatively independent. There seems also, in this instance, to be some application of the principle of correlated growth; for while the males and the sterile females are said to drop their horns in November, the mothers retain theirs until after the birth of the fawns in the May following. The small horns in many female ruminants, whether originally acquired by the males, as seems probable, or otherwise, are useful for defence and generally retained for life. They are sustained at very trifling expense.

But on the principle that "sports" or sudden and considerable changes of structure very rarely occur in a state of nature, yet are frequent, both with animals and plants under cultivation, chiefly because of changed conditions and abundance of food, it is not impossible that very thrifty males may have acquired variations suddenly or in a much shorter time than Mr. Darwin supposes. Whether originally acquired gradually by very . small increments of growth, from individual to individual, or by a more rapid growth in one or many animals. and transmitted to offspring, the tendency to vary from the species seems to arise almost wholly in the male line. Nothing analogous to these extra structural modifications seems to originate with females, except as required by particular feminine functions. In insects there is often a curious development of instruments for sawing, boring, etc., that the eggs may be deposited in places where they can obtain the proper nutriment. With higher beings, there are various other useful differentiations to special ends ; but females *originate* no useless or apparently useless appendages. Where they *inherit* these, this may be required by the laws of correlation, and by sexual equilibrium. It is probable that each sex must

always develop the characters of the other to the full
extent to which this is permitted by vigor of constitution and the laws of correlated growth.   Thus the
ruminants have not generally developed the characters
of the opposite sex to a very large extent.   The over-
burdened mothers have little energy to spare in
becoming pugnacious, in enjoying rapid and long
marches, or in growing worse than useless ornaments.   The males, with their unlike habits, can
perhaps benefit the race better by developing
strength, spirit, and courage, than through the growth
of parental anxiety and tenderness.   Not until the
two sets of characters so far coalesce in offspring
that the one set directly balances the other, and both
unfold together to some degree in the same sex, can
either inherit from the other ; but the females may
retain the traits of the mother and the males of the
father.

With the continued evolution of each, in process of
time there arise more and more points of mutual
adjustment, of complex adaptations ; then one or both
sexes can begin to develop the characters of the other.
Whenever brilliantly-colored male birds have acquired

something of maternal habits, tastes, and impulses, conversely the females seem always to have acquired some counterbalancing weight of male characters. They are large in relative size, are brilliantly colored, are active and quarrelsome, or are a little of all these together. The large majority of birds illustrate this law. Many of the females seem to have become brilliantly colored, probably, as Mr. Darwin supposes, through paternal inheritance. Humming birds are a good example. The females have become magnificent in color; and the males have some share of domestic traits. All classes of carnivorous animals are also illustrations of the same law. The sexes are colored much alike; sometimes, as with the spotted leopard and the royal tiger, there is really no difference in the beauty and brilliancy of the hue. Both sexes are strong, fierce, and full of excitability and of courage ; both seem equally intelligent and almost equally fond of their offspring. Even the South African lion has some share of the same feminine instincts which have been acquired by his kindred; and the females are beautiful and spirited.

The more complex structure of the female

mammalia may be offset against the extra male size
—the difference of the development beginning from
the first initiation of fœtal life and continuing until
each sex has attained its full growth.   The excess of
nutrition directly devoted to reproduction by the one
sex, is quite compensated for by the indirect force
expended in maintaining the extra bulk and strength
devoted to hunting.   Females sometimes inherit
male characters, as horns by the reindeer, when no
direct balance of female characters seems to be correspondingly inherited by the males in return.   But
the relation of secondary characters are not always
self-evident.   The laws of growth and of inheritance are extremely complex and not well understood.
Just as the male sometimes develops what seem to
be positively inconvenient and very wasteful characters, and acquires the habit of expending an
immense amount of energy in mere sport and recreation, so, when the female inherits his peculiarities, he
may perhaps merely go on in the same direction as
before, as an offset; some now inexplicable good
being the final outcome of the whole.   It certainly
shows a much greater redundancy of force to

originate variations than merely to *inherit* them ; and
it must not be forgotten that males and females are
analogous in all details of fundamental development.
The respiration, the nervous system, the bony skele-
ton, the generative organs, though all more or less
modified in each sex, are advanced together ; so that
the whole organism of each species is in direct sympathy with its complemental organism in the other
sex. It becomes very probable, therefore, *that all
extra characters have some balancing function to
perform,* and are of positive utility to the race.

I have associated vivid color with warmth and
activity of character, and with the ultimate structure
of related atoms in the organism. The soil in which
a plant grows will influence its color ; a scarcity or
an abundance of the same food will deaden or
brighten the coat of an animal ; a stimulating diet or
exciting beverages will heighten the complexion of
man. But all characters, hereditary or acquired by
habit, have some tendency to transmit themselves to
offspring. Color, whatever its origin, partakes of the
universal tendency to self-adjusting symmetry. It
seems inevitable that it should be aggregated in

orderly arrangements ; that it should tend to definite lines and other symmetrical markings, or should draw together in spots, shaded and variously tinted. What are the intensely, the wonderfully-colored eyes in all animals but one illustration of this? The marvellous organic eye shows not merely the attractive tendency which concentrates and graduates color; but the vivid depths of it, which gather here as about a pivot, seem to be related both to the subtle, beautiful intensity of vision as a psychical experience, and to the objective action of light in color-forming. The warmest and brightest of the sensations has acquired its appropriate outward symbol. Related as sight is to rapid molecular motion, raised to the white-heat intensity of light, how could it be otherwise?

I believe it will be found that there is no highly-colored substance anywhere in nature which is not directly associated either with a high state of warmth or of light. The little sharp-angled, polished reflectors of light, such as are found on the scales of fish and on wings and plumes, may be only mechanical modifications to effect simply mechanical results.

This would not militate against the theory, but would help rather to fortify it still farther. Those various minute mechanical contrivances, which throw back the light like little sheets of many-colored flames, may be only so many modified prisms, each one adjusted to some element of the light itself. Nature can manufacture them only in connection with the sunlight or in water permeated with sunshine. As darkness seems to obliterate color to our sight, so none of those relations of atoms on which the effect of color depends seem to be possible where there is neither light nor warmth.

Chemical combinations are attended both by heat and color, with some evident close relation between the two. Many precious stones are both very highly and most symmetrically colored. The often wondrously-shaded ocelli or eye-like spots on butterflies' wings ; which have become so magnificent on the feathers of the peacock ; seem to have developed like all other aggregations. Scarcely less striking are the shaded petals of a flower or the deep red on a maiden's lips and transiently blooming cheeks. There is the same symmetry in an agate, in all the deeply-dyed precious

stones, and in all the many colors of the inorganic
world. The same symmetry is developed in the color-
less crystal—in short, in every form and in every action in nature, organic and inorganic. It is obviously
the result of balanced activities, of balanced tensions ;
which are but attractions and repulsions crystallized
or in static form. In the organic cell these tensions
are at once fixed and mobile ; for the organism is an
endless process through which kindred matter and
force are assimilated, utilized, and rejected, the whole
tending always and in all ways towards a wider and
higher perfection. That the marvellously shaded ball
and socket ornaments of the Argus pheasant, and the
brilliancy of birds, and beasts, and flowers, have all
been acquired gradually, seems to be as certain as
that there has been evolution in all other directions.
The whole structure of a living organism may be
regarded as expressly designed, not only for continual
change, but for the possibility of continual improvement.

Neither can one doubt that the love of the beautiful has been always developing with other sentient
faculties in all races of beings, or that animals are

attracted by agreeable colors and other ornaments; but that sexual selection of the most beautiful has played the conspicuous part in evolution which Mr. Darwin assigns to it, is at least questionable.

If no æsthetic sentiment had been developed anywhere in the lowest or the highest being, it seems certain that color and form must both have been evolved, more slowly, perhaps, yet certainly very much as they have been evolved in the past ages. One atom of colored matter must have tended always to attract another: this tendency would increase from generation to generation, as the greater complexity of conditions gradually evolved the whole structure. Thus birds, insects, and fishes, living much in the sunlight, if they could acquire the first rudiments of brilliant coloring, would of necessity go on towards perfection in this acquirement. Like everywhere attracts its like. This necessity lies in the related constitution of atoms, of all things. By a similar innate necessity, the nervous system, with its brain and its related physical evolution, are also perfected; the *appreciation of symmetry and of color* springing into activity with the other faculties.

That sentient and unsentient forces are related, is unquestionable ; that they are mutually convertible, has not yet been proved : but that all modes of physical force are convertible among themselves, and that thought can be exchanged for feeling, and feeling for thought, are matters of demonstration. It is equally certain that if an organism is overworked physically, all mental powers are so related to this organism that they must lie comparatively dormant. With a disordered brain there is no sane thought, no beautiful sensation, emotion, or purpose. As the higher, more complex brain has been gradually evolved, higher modes of thinking, feeling, and acting have become possible ; have become to men obligatory.

But the brain is only one part of the whole nervous system, and this nervous system is differently modified in the sexes of every species, in correlation with all the other differentiations of sex. The brain has everywhere been developed in conjunction with the general structure ; but the differentiation of brain and other nerve-structure in male and female has kept pace with the general and special differences of the sexes. Mental traits have universally differed as fun-

damentally in the two sexes as the organisms through
which they were evolved. Apparently there is a correlated balance of psychical as of physical qualities.

In the language of Professor Agassiz, " Generation
is based upon that harmonious antagonism between
the sexes, that contrast between the male and the
female element, that at once divides and unites the
whole Animal Kingdom. And although this exchange
of influence is not kept up by an equality of numeric
relations * * * yet I firmly believe that this numerical distribution, however unequal it may seem to us,
is not without its ordained accuracy and balance.
He who has assigned its place to every leaf in the
thickest forest, according to an arithmetical law which
prescribes to each its allotted share of room on the
branch where it grows, will not have distributed
animal life with less care and regularity."

A " pre-established harmony " is found to exist in
the innate constitution of the ultimate atoms of
substance. Under stimulating conditions, they can
and do co-operate to produce definite arithmetical results. One of the higher results is organization—
still another the evolution of organizations. This

is always accompanied, at least in the higher stages, by the unfolding of psychical powers ; by the final development of intellectual and moral natures. Every theory of evolution ends in the evolving of a conscious individuality. Whether certain potentially sentient and indestructible atoms, dating from the beginning of the present established order, have been able to develop their psychical possibilities through organization ; or, whether all psychical powers, arising solely in and through organization, are destroyed again through its dissolution (except in so far as they are perpetuated in posterity), are questions not easy of solution ; concerning which there may be unsettled or differing opinions. But that the relations of organic forces are so balanced and adapted that they evolve male and female, each sex the complemental equivalent of the other in every order of being, producing a division of elements to be reunited in every new individual of the species, is a fact so perpetually illustrated at every step of the progressive way upward, that if attention is called strongly in this direction, science must surely enable us all to see eye to eye in this matter. Whether

" the male and the female element " arise solely through an early division of functions, or whether the potentialities of sex pre-exist in the mental atoms, we may never be able to determine. Nor is it important to do so. Mr. Spencer's masterly reasoning as to the redistribution of matter and force in every organism consequent upon the action of unlike external forces, applied to the unlike organic forces which determine sex, will show that in either case the differentiations of male and female must be complete and total, extending to all attributes physiological and psychological.

Now as to the balance of qualities in men and women. The special adaptations and economies of Nature are in active operation from the first. The future woman is not destined to attain to the size of the man ; Nature therefore adds atom to atom in the new organism with dainty care, rejecting the unfit more rigidly than with the boy. But the work is done with equal energy ; for within a smaller compass there is to be wrought out a structure, part for part the analogue of his, not less perfect in every detail, but supplemented by yet other organs which are unique—the male developing only their merest rudiments. This smaller, more complex structure must therefore be the more delicately elaborated.

Silk-growers in Europe are said to determine the sexes of the larva by weight. The human species might be systematically distinguished in the same way, at any time from the earliest fœtal life up to a dozen or fourteen years; and again from sixteen or eighteen to forty-five or fifty. But the *relative size* of the sexes is reversed between the silk-worm and man. The worm, having but two functions, growth and reproduction, an extra amount of nutrition here becomes pre-eminently important. Natural selection determines that the sex which most directly contributes to the wellbeing of the race shall take precedence in favorable conditions. Human beings, with their multitude of functions, are surrounded by a complexity of conditions. Science has not determined what series of pre-potencies is sufficient to decide the sex.

But when nearly grown, the girl, who has never before equalled her brother in size, suddenly overtakes or even outstrips him in bulk. Why? Because,

the work of organic development completed, the
simpler task of adding like increments can be rapidly
accomplished. Nature has already begun the process
of storing up force, which is on demand, should it
be needed in the growth of offspring. If it is not
needed, there shortly begins the periodical work of
elimination. If it is needed, it is appropriated as
provided. It appears that the appropriation is not
made—is not intended to be made, at least—at
the expense of the mother's own proper supply
of nutritive force, or of force devoted to any other
purpose in the economy of the feminine organism,
with its totality of functions. An elaborate,
highly-developed reproductive system, with its own
proper and complete nutritive relations, has been
evolved as one special function of the feminine
organism.

The nutrition which is continually and functionally stored up for reproductive processes can doubtless in any exigency—so close is the relation of every
function to every other—be diverted from its appropriate use. When the system is over-taxed, under-
fed, impaired by sickness or by any other course, this

provision may be drawn upon for general purposes ; yet the abnormal diversion will be accompanied by the same kind of disturbance as follows the perversion of any other nutriment. When the brain is excessively used, it robs the body, which is weakened in proportion ; or if muscle is over-exercised, the brain suffers ; or if there is an over-tax of the reproductive functions, the whole organism is depleted. Physiologists now admit that every great nervous centre must be maintained in balanced activity, that it may draw its proper nutritive supply. The digestive organs themselves must work and rest alternately, so must every nerve and member ; for all act in correlation. The feminine functions find their place in the system, co-ordinated with all the others ; equally normal, equally healthful, and even more fundamental. Periodicity of function, maternity, lactation, all being organically provided for, each in relation to the other, neither should cause the least disturbance to health ; neither should subtract anything from the general functions of nutrition, and all should add, as all other balanced activity does, to a larger vigor both of mind and body. The legitimate use of any and of every faculty is strengthening, not exhausting. How can there exist a more fundamental antagonism between individual wellbeing and the balanced exercise of one function, than between it and any or every other function? They have all grown together in mutual adaptation. A disturbance of one is the disturbance of all.

The girl attains physical maturity earlier than the boy. May not this be because there is less to mature, because all the processes, smaller in quantity, yet driven with equal force, have been accelerated in activity. Her circulation and respiration are more rapid. So are her mental processes. Why? Let science investigate the whole subject quantitatively. It may be found, process for process, in detail and in totality, that the average woman is equal to the average man. By all means let the sexes be studied mathematically.

At present, under the prevailing theory of the proper weakness and helplessness of the girl, we forget that food and oxygen are measures of force, and exercise largely the measure of appetite and digestion. The girl, starved by conventionality in body and

mind, hinders the evolution of the race, or entails upon
it a weak and unbalanced constitution. One writer
says: "The monster who is in the way of woman's
progress is not man, so much as the idle women who
want somebody else to think for them, work for
them, do for them, and even dress them." True; but
the great underlying cause of all is a false theory
that, because women are to be the mothers of the
race, therefore they are not to be the thinkers or the
pioneers in enterprise. This ancient dogma enfeebles
one class of women and degrades the other. We believe in a fairly equal division of duties between men
and women; but not that the wife of a laboring man,
who accepts ten hours of daily toil as his share of
family duty, is bound by her duty to spend twenty-
four hours among the pots and the children, with no
absolute rest and without fitting recreation. If woman's sole responsibility is of the domestic type, one
class will be crushed by it, and the other throw it off
as a badge of poverty. The poor man's motto,
"Woman's work is never done," leads inevitably to its
antithesis—ladies' work is never begun.

Let us suppose that natural selection has continually averaged the duty of the sexes to offspring, by modification and adjustment of each organism to its appropiate functions. At maturity, then, males and females would be true equivalents, each equally well fortified to meet its own responsibilities. Woman's share of duties must involve direct nutrition, man's indirect nutrition. She should be able to bear and nourish their young children, at a cost of energy equal to the amount expended by him as household provider. Beyond this, if human justice is to supplement Nature's provisions, all family duties must be shared equitably, in person or by proxy. Work, alternated with needful rest, is the salvation of man or woman. Far be it from me to encourage one human being as an idler! But *in the scientific distribution of work*, the males, not the females, must be held primarily responsible for the proper *cooking of food*, as for the *production* of it. Since we cannot thrive on the raw materials, like the lower animals, culinary processes must be *allied to indirect nutrition.*

In the progress of functions, the human mother must contribute much more towards the direct sus-

tenance of offspring than any class of inferior beings.
For many months before and for many months after
its birth, her system must elaborate the entire food
of her child. Its growth and activity are supplemental to her own, and are as absolutely at her expense
as is the growth of her own right arm. But Nature
has provided for that by giving her a smaller frame of
her own, and less disposition to great activity per-
sonally, with less need of it in the interest of perfect
health. Nature is just enough ; but men and women
must comprehend and accept her suggestions. For
the best fulfilment of maternal duties, the mother
must have comfortable surroundings provided for her
without a large personal tax on her own energies.
Therefore it seems to me to be scientifically
demonstrable that fathers are equitably bound to
contribute indirect sustenance to offspring in the
shape of good edible food for the mother. To this
we might add ready-made clothing and fires lighted
on cold winter mornings !

Undoubtedly, in the division of the many complex
duties of life, it may be equitable and decidedly best
in many households that the wives should be respon-

sible for the family cooking and sewing ; yet it should be understood that they both belong more properly to the category of masculine function, and pertain to the indirect nurture of the youthful scions of the household. Every nursing mother, in the midst of her little dependent brood, has far more right to whine, sulk, or scold, as temperament dictates, because beefsteak and coffee are not prepared for her and exactly to her taste, than any man ever had or ever can have during the present stage of human evolution. Other things equal—during the whole child-bearing age, at least—if family necessity compels to extra hours of toil or care, these must belong to the husband, never to the wife. The interests of their children *must not be sacrificed* by her over-exhaustion, even though she were willing and eager for the sacrifice of herself.

On the other hand, as highly complex beings, women must be taught to exercise all their functions, that they may develop and strengthen all their faculties healthfully and symmetrically. *A regimen of sofas* must be as utterly demoralizing as would be a regimen of soft bread and milk, appropriate enough to the yearling baby. Mental torpor must be still more fatal, and aimless restlessness of body or mind, if possible, worse than either. In brief, then, let woman take part in any human enterprise which is at once attractive, feasible, *compatible with a fair division of family duties*, and thoroughly honorable in its character. Let her choose her own work and learn to do it in her own way, instructed only to maintain the natural balance of all her many admirably-appointed faculties ; that she and her descendants after her may be alike subject to the laws of health. If anybody's *brain* requires to be sacrificed to those two Molochs, sewing-machine and cooking-stove, it is not hers ! Nature's highest law is evolution, and no hereditary evolution is possible except through the prolonged maternal supervention.

The mother may transmit male characters to her son ; but there is much evidence that a correlative feminine equivalent must first have found some place in her own nature. The pollen of a widely alien plant cannot fertilize a seed, nor can the wisest man bequeath intellect to children through the agency of a weak-minded or characterless mother.

The nervous system, in every convolution of the

brain, in every fibre of the extended network of mobile tissue, through which all mental activity must find expression, has been necessarily modified in correspondence with the feminine organism and its maternal functions. Masculine mental character, doubtless, cannot be inherited by female descendants. But what shall hinder that an equivalent mentality, or rather an equivalent organic nerve-system, through which mind can work, be inherited alike by sons and daughters? Nothing. Nothing can hinder such an inheritance. Nothing can prevent its fullest subsequent development into active force, except such persistent dawdling habits as may rob a young girl of appetite, digestion, energy to profit by the steady unfolding of all best gifts.

But feminine deficiencies, when acquired, are entailed as heirlooms to the sons as to the daughters. Thus has Nature been forced to maintain the average equality of sex. Defrauded womanhood, as unwittingly to herself as to man, has been everywhere avenged for the system of arrogant repression under which she has always stifled hitherto; the human race, forever retarding its own advancement, because it could not recognize and promote a genuine, broad, and healthful equilibrium of the sexes. Of course the son cannot inherit feminine characters without modification. He is heir only to the fatal *equivalent* of every weakness fostered in his female ancestors—gifts not always patent to the world as a direct maternal legacy. But how is it possible that any scientific reasoner can fail to see that like must beget like—the diverging lines, male and female, converging again in the child. It is not each added to the other, but the one balancing the other with a force as feeble as the feeblest.

Fortunately, Nature is so tenacious of her ends, that a vast amount of inherent feminine vitality must persist, though never voluntarily exercised. Organic processes will tend to utilize the latent energies, and a doll or a drudge, with qualities which might have made a noble woman, may possibly become the mother of very noble children. But it must be sheer folly to believe that the offspring of such an one will not be defrauded of the increase which should revert to them from the exercise of parental talent.

There is a special directness in feminine perception which is in curious correspondence with the
organic functions. The rapid intuitions with which
women are credited, are simply direct perceptions.
Their minds incline to the *direct reading* of all facts,
from the simplest to the most complex and involved.
They are quick to detect the dawning sentiments of
a little child, or to divine the disguised opinions of
the consummate man or woman of the world ; to catch
the details of a leaf at sight, or to gather at a glance
the salient points of a landscape. Some man says, he
never made his toilsome way up to any vantage-
ground without finding a woman there in advance of
him. The statement may be more than a compli-
ment. A woman finds the natural lay of the land
almost unconsciously ; and not feeling it incumbent
on her to be guide and philosopher to any successor,
she takes little pains to mark the route by which she
is making her ascent. John Stuart Mill, the life-long
student of philosophy, must be credited with sincerity
when he so earnestly reiterates that his wife was
often his leader in abstract thinking, his superior in
finding the truths after which they were both search-

ing. He was emphatically a logician ; she had quick perceptive powers. The one was a strong man, the other a strong woman.

We may argue with Mr. Spencer, that the primitive women as subjects, weak and dependent, would learn to watch the rising impulses of their rough guardians, in order to detect the dawning pleasure or displeasure, and shape their own conduct accordingly —thus accounting for the growth of subtle feminine perceptions. But every wary savage would be about equally impelled to study his rivals, his chief, and other superiors of his tribe. In his wider dealings with the outer world, he would be still more strongly impelled to watch sharply, that he might take advantage of each new possibility, and guard against every unknown danger. His powers of observation were thus wonderfully sharpened ; yet neither this savage nor his male descendants have developed the direct insight that delights to penetrate beneath the surface without the aid of logic and circumlocution.

The *indirect method* of acquiring truth by reasoning—evolving it first in consciousness, testing it by the laws of thought, seems to be as characteristic of the male mind as intuition is of the female. Apparently a man can never content himself to look at anything persistently till he is quite satisfied that he can see and comprehend some few or many of its bearings. He must turn aside to reason about it, to con it over in the light of his own mental atmosphere. Since the earliest dawn of the historic ages, the current working machinery of masculine investigators has been a truly wonderful array of clever and ingenious hypotheses.

Women might have invented less cleverly, and, trying never so diligently, might have succeeded in discovering no greater, possibly a much less, body of knowledge ; but it is entirely certain that, if impelled to do so, they would have gone to work with much less indirection. Scientific philosophy is beginning to comprehend that if one would learn anything, the best text-book is the thing itself ; if he would follow out its ever-widening relations, he must find these also as they exist and where they exist. Nature is found to have a logic of her own, which is quite equal to masculine reasoning for infallibility, with the additional advantage that Nature invariably gets all the facts, near and remote, into her premises, to the exclusion of everything else ; making a most important difference frequently in the conclusions. Now, if it could be shown that the most primary instincts of women are objective rather than subjective, and lead them outward into direct intuition, it must become evident that they would bring new modes of force and fresh methods of inquiry into every department of research.

There is a convenient hypothesis that the intellect of the female, among all the higher orders of being, has acquired a development intermediate between the young of the species and the males, as their bodies and brains are intermediate in size. It is a theory closely akin to the time-honored assumption that the male is the normal type of his species; the female the modification to a special end. Also, it is nearly allied to any scheme of Evolution which believes that progress is affected chiefly through the acquirement and transmission of masculine characters.

But, likening evolution to a chain—each side of the link advancing and diverging, but meeting again in the junction of the link succeeding—we must allow a due share to the two halves of the connected whole. The amount of psychical development in the female may or may not have progressed into more advanced life ; but it must be represented by equivalent stages in every new link of the series. The wonderful instincts and skill of insect mothers manifested in the provision made for their offspring, the superior ingenuity of the mother-birds in nest-building, the greater parental sagacity and affection of the higher female animals manifest in the defense and care of their young, we have already seen to be at least as high in the psychical scale, and of as much value to the race, as the superior warlike and passional instincts of their males. It remains only to compare the psychical powers of the sexes in the human race.

It may be demonstrated that the nervous system, which is the primary organ of mind, has acquired greater *special development* in the woman than in the man The differentiation between woman and child is much greater *in kind* than between man and child ; the difference in *quantity* remains with the man. The female organism, selected during countless ages to elaborate much larger amounts of reproductive elements, in correspondence with this fact, has been progressively furnished with a graduated supply of blood-vessels, feeders of the special organs, and all these have their closely-attendant nerves. Thus, a progressively modified nervous system has kept pace in growth and development with the evolutions of the reproductive functions, till, in the mammalia, there is more than one nervous plexus well developed in adult females which is only rudimentary in the young and in the mature males. Now, if these nerve-ganglia and their added ramifications must be considered as partially automatic, they are yet allied to consciousness ; exerting a profound influence over the whole sentient nature, and capable of elevating or depressing the entire mental activity. The brain is not, and cannot be, the sole or complete organ of thought and feeling.

Herbert Spencer's theory, that, as the male exhales relatively more carbonic acid than the female, this fact must be taken as the measure of oxygen consumed, and therefore of the amount of force evolved, takes no account of a differentiation of functions. The feminine system has other methods of eliminating waste matter along with the surplus nutritive elements, and perhaps even with the waste from the embryonic processes. Besides, at all ages of a woman's life, the skin and other tissues must be the more active in expelling refuse matter.

Conventionality has indeed curtailed feminine force by hindering healthful and varied activity ; but Nature is continually devising compensations for that loss. When, from deficient action of mind or body, there is less appetite, less food consumed, and less strength evolved, there is also less expended. And whenever there is an excessive drain on any set of functions, psychical or physical, the feminine economy has made it easier to restore the balance than with men, for whom there is no equal organic provision. It seems to be an offset to his superior strength and activity, and it gives to the weaker and less active of the two the greater relative power of endurance, and the ability to bear a much wider departure from normal conditions comparatively unharmed. Therefore loss of sleep, loss of food, great fatigue, or great indolence of mind or body, are less exhausting to the female organism than to the male—

a much-needed provision, especially in the ruder barbaric ages, when might was the most easily-recognized patent of right. It will be also an excellent additional safeguard to the feminine brain-workers of a more intellectual era.

Worse than useless it must be to overlook the wide fundamental differentiations of the totality of functions in the mature man and woman. Utterly futile must it be to set bounds and limits to either, without taking into full account the nicely-adjusted balance to the entire organism; fitting it to solve its own problems of duty and destiny, and to gauge its own capacities unhindered.

We have been told that Nature has intended no loss of feminine nutritive elements, but that she has blundered in her scheme, falling into the bungling device of helplessly allowing a great rythmical system of sheer waste and improvidence. As well insist that Nature *never intended* a child to play! All the young things which she has made do frisk about endlessly, wasting an untold amount of force in aimless activity; though it can be no part of the frugal scheme of things to tolerate such reckless waste.

An organism that had been most carefully adapted to assimilate more nutritive force than it can possibly need for the highest healthful exercise of its own personal functions, must be as really benefited by elaborating the amounts for reproductive purposes, not thus utilized, as the child is by play, which serves no other end than the exercise of its growing muscles. Nature, though a rigid economist, is never penny-wise and pound-foolish. Steadily mindful of the great fact that the higher the rise in the scale of being, the more all nutritive functions must be subordinated and in adaptation to higher, more active modes of force ; Nature has adjusted a self-balancing equilibrium in the feminine organism which reduces all disturbance arising from maternal functions to the smallest amount. Every faculty, physical or psychical, when in vigorous health, may be exercised moderately, not only without injury, but with positive advantage both to mother and child. Could any better system be devised ? As the mother of six children, I may be permitted to doubt this, to profess entire satisfaction with the admirable present scheme, to offer the testimony of experience to its possible perfection as a working system, and to reiterate my conviction that Nature is an absolutely impartial mother to her sons and her daughters.

In all these related modifications, there is a wider differentiation between the woman and the child than between the man and the child. It becomes evident that the entire mental character must be greatly influenced by these provisions, many and various, for the redistribution of force. The nervous system is the brain system. Its greater special development in relation with the reproductive functions would probably involve a commensurate less development in the brain. Brain development would be itself modified. The mental character of men and women must therefore be differentiated, as they act through fundamentally differentiated nervous systems.

Possibly, in adaptation to her smaller size, the woman may have a greater relative development of nerve-tissue than the man. The facts need careful investigation. Science has not determined in regard to it. I do not know that it has ever sought to do so, that it has ever raised the question as to woman's actual equality, or as to her relative equality in the total of nerve-tissue and of nerve-force. It has sought to compare the relative size and power of the average male and female brain ; but the brain-system is no more shut up within the cranium than the great system of blood-vessels is shut up within the heart. Psychical action can no more be fairly measured or estimated in its modes of activity by the size and action of the brain alone, than the amount and rate of the circulation of the blood could be learned from the heart alone. Harvey discovered the wonderful facts of the blood-circulation by tracing it in its whole complicated round through the system. The neurologists have discovered how the nerves act in conducting nerve force to and fro from the nerve-centres, not by watching the brain alone, but by comprehensive investigation of the whole co-operative nervous system. And yet I cannot learn that any scientist has proposed to estimate the psychical force of males and females on any other basis than that of the relative size of their brains and muscles. This mode of inference may suffice in comparing men with the lower animals, because the whole nervous system in its development keeps pace with the increasing size and complexity of the cranial mass; but the male nervous system is progressively differentiated from the female in the rising chain of species. In the human race the difference has become so important that when it is wholly ignored, and the comparison made by taking only two of the factors—size of brain and size of body—great injustice must be done to the female whose nervous system has become the more complex and is not aggregated to an equal extent within the cranium.

Low organisms and fœtal animals have no hearts, yet they have a circulation; and animals with the brains removed may have the remnant of a nervous system still in action. The brain is necessary to sensation, but so are the special sense organs. The brain is the great seat of the emotions; but the related nerve system, which is woven into the heart, which is specially modified and developed in the feminine organism, seems to be as influential upon the emotions as the senses are to sensation. The brain thinks; but how it thinks is as much determined by the kind and quality of the nerve-system, which is in co-operation with it, as its sensations are determined by special senses.

This is not asserting that the mind is nothing without its organism. I believe profoundly in the existence of the ˙sentient, personal, indestructible atom,.as distinguished from its organism with which it co-operates ; but it is mind instinct in the whole living system ; the network of nerves is the direct medium of its psychical development and manifestation.

It is currently known that the emotional and intellectual processes in woman are *more closely in relation* than in man. A more direct and frequent interchange seems to have been established between them. Thought and feeling work together more inseparably than in man. This is a fact learned by everyday experience, learned by comparing the masculine and feminine methods of working. Comparative anatomy of their modified nervous systems must suggest corresponding facts of structure.

Women's thoughts are impelled by their feelings. Hence the sharp-sightedness, the direct insight, the quick perceptions ; hence also their warmer prejudices and more unbalanced judgments, and their infrequent use of the masculine methods of ratiocination. In this the child is like the woman. Its feelings directly impel its actions. The immediate sensation or perception seems also to be the impelling power of the savage and of all animal instincts. Call it automatic activity if you will ; yet the incident force is real feeling, is perception, is intelligence, and is, as I believe, ordinarily accompanied by volition which has acquired more or less development towards such mastery of the situation that it may choose or reject on its own sovereign responsibility.

The will, if free will is a possible function, must be subject to evolution, like all other psychical development ; and in will-power the woman has never shown herself to be deficient. It is a strong mark of distinction between her mental processes and those of the child, or the animal with strongly-developed special instincts. The woman, as much or more than any other being, man not excepted, is able to put aside personal feeling and personal interest, to follow the lead of her impersonal judgment.

But although thought and feeling are more nearly related in the child and woman than in the man, and though the latter, in his mature development, is thus differentiated from the child, I hold that the woman's mode of thinking and feeling is still more differentiated from that of childhood. The child is pre-eminently self-centred in all his psychical development. The law of grab is the primal law of infancy. "I want it," "I feel like it," is the impelling mainspring of its activity. It knows nothing of duty, and cares nothing for the interests or rights of others, till it is taught these things educationally.

Now the woman is not constitutionally self-centred in thought or feeling. Her sympathies have been functionally carried forward into an objective channel. Her instincts impel her to self-forgetfulness in thinking and acting for her children, and inherited habit has developed and extended the tendency to whatever person or subject demands her care and occupies her thoughts. Thus her nature must have been tending for many ages towards the objective in thought, the impersonal in feeling; towards the abstract in principle. Of course, human development is complex, subject to many cross complications, which neutralize each other. There are women of mature years who never, in mental development, get beyond childhood, with all its absorbing self-centredness or selfishness. We may charitably hope that their volitions, like their perceptive powers, are little more than rudimentary. There are men who have developed the transmitted feminine qualities, and by a more indirect route have become the most disinterested of their species. But, class for class, as the race now is, it is apparently easier for women to practice self-negation than for men, and more normal for them to develop an objective or perceptive intellect than a subjective or ratiocinative intellect. There are certainly as many points of antithesis between childhood and the highest female development, as between childhood and the highest male development.

The mature woman is not incapable of appreciating the most highly complex fact or the most abstract principle. She learns easily to recognize all these, with their relative bearings; and can perceive existing relations as readily as she sees the objects related. Her outlook is forward and backward, with as wide a reach in either direction as man's. That she is not his peer in all intellectual and moral capabilities, cannot at least be very well proved until she is

allowed an equally untrammelled opportunity to test
her own strength.   It would be possible to carry on a
running comparison in detail ; to laud her untested
powers, prophesying her future success in execu-
tive ability, in abstract thinking, or in physical and
moral science ; but I have no wish to do so.   All
doors are now measurably open to her.   Whatever
her hand finds to do, let her do it with her might, in
demonstration of her capacity.

Morally certain it is that she will neither forego,
nor desire to forego, her domestic relations ; nor will
the average woman seek to evade an equitable share
of the burdens or disabilities of her station, or shrink
from sharing honorably all the many duties which
arise within the home-life.   Evolution has given and
is still giving to woman an increasing complexity of
development which cannot find a legitimate field for
the exercise of all its powers within the household.
There is a broader, not a higher, life outside, which
she is impelled to enter, taking some share also in its
responsibilities.

This need in no wise interfere with the everyday
comforts, the fostering mental influences, and the

moral sanctities of the home, nor with the highest
good of the olive-plants which will continue to bud
and blossom in every household. The restless, nervous woman of to-day may rather be expected to
attain a more contented and well-poised temperament
with the more symmetrical development. She will
find opportunity to convert some of the smothered
discontent, fostered by superfluous sentiment with
inaction, into the energy of wider thought, purpose,
and achievement.

If Evolution, as applied to sex, teaches any one
lesson plainer than another, it is the lesson that the
monogamic marriage is the basis of all progress.
Nature, who everywhere holds her balances with even
justice, asks only that every husband and wife shall
co-operate to develop her most dilligently-selected
characters. When she has endowed any woman with
special talents, the balanced development of such a
character requires the amplest exercise of these pre-
dominant gifts. Any prevailing tendency is itself
evidence that the entire organism is adjusted to promote its superior activity. If it is a quality, just,
honorable, desirable to be attained by the race, to

hinder its highest development is to retard the normal rate of human progress; to interfere unwarrantably with a fundamental law of evolution. No theory of unfitness, no form of conventionality, can have the right to suppress any excellence which Nature has seen fit to evolve. Men and women, in search of the same ends, must co-operate in as many heterogeneous pursuits as the present development of the race enables them both to recognize and appreciate.

THE ALLEGED ANTAGONISM BE-
TWEEN GROWTH AND REPRO-
DUCTION.

THE supposed law of inverse relations between
growth and reproduction was first announced, I think,
by Dr. Carpenter, but adopted independently by Mr.
Spencer, whose elaborate, forcible arguments have
done much to convince many physiologists that a
principle so well established may be accepted without
further question. But the underlying facts are so
various, complex, and unsolved, it is by no means
impossible, or even improbable, that some new element yet to be introduced into the premises may
partially modify or even reverse the necessary logical
conclusion.

The following are Mr. Spencer's main points,
gathered from his "Principles of Biology," and stated
in his own condensed language: "Genesis, under
every form, is a process of negative or positive disin-

tegration, and is thus essentially opposed to that process of integration which is one element of individual evolution." *

" When the excess of assimilative power is diminishing in such a way as to indicate its approaching disappearance, it becomes needful, for the maintenance of the species, that this excess shall be turned to the production of new individuals ; since, did growth continue until this excess disappeared through the complete balancing of assimilation and expenditure, the production of new individuals would be either impossible or fatal to the parent." †

"We cannot help admitting that the proportion between the aggregative and separative tendencies must in each case determine the relation between the increase in bulk of the individual and the increase of the race in numbers." ‡

Up to this point one may freely admit the antagonistic relations alleged ; but when, in his article on " The Psychology of the Sexes," Mr. Spencer asserts that "a somewhat earlier arrest of individual development in women than in men is necessitated by the

* Vol. I., p. 216.　　† P. 237.　　‡ Vol. II., p. 426.

reservation of vital force to meet the cost of reproduction," there are so many not yet discounted conditions to be considered that the position cannot be regarded as satisfactorily sustained. *There is* the "earlier arrest" of physical growth; the "rather smaller growth of the nervo-muscular system;" the much longer nutritive tax demanded for the nourishment of fœtal and infant life; the "somewhat less of general power or massiveness" in feminine mental manifestations; *there may be,* "beyond this, a perceptible falling short in those two faculties, intellectual and emotional, which are the latest products of human evolution— the power of abstract reasoning, and that most abstract of the emotions, the sentiment of justice." It does not therefore follow that these results, any or all of them are deductions made from the "cost of reproduction." Force modified and readjusted is not force subtracted or destroyed.

The smaller nervo-muscular system, and the diminished power or massiveness of mental action, may be supposed to arise as direct results of the larger nutritive cost of maternity. But the earlier arrest of physical growth may or may not be coupled with an earlier arrest of mental development ; and one or both of these may offer to us very marked illustrations—not of process prematurely cut short to be handed over to offspring—but of process quickened by other related antecedents, and therefore more rapidly completed. This need not involve loss or transfer of individual force to offspring ; but, rather, a modified system of the transfer of substance and force from the environment to the reproductive functions and their products.

If it could be shown that men or women who are the parents of many children have thereby lost something of individual power, we might then be forced to admit that the greater cost related to the reproductive system in women must be at their personal expense, not at the expense of the nutriment which they assimilate and eliminate.

The weaknesses resulting from a too early or an excessive tax of functions belong to a distinct class of considerations. I assume that every balanced constitutional activity, though including loss of nutritive elements, is yet a normal aid to constitutional strength. Every action, physical or psychical, involves either integration or disintegration ; every use of faculty belongs to the latter class. There is no more antagonism between growth and reproduction than between growth and thought, growth and muscular activity, growth and breathing. The antagonism is only that of action and reaction, which are but two phases of the same process—opposing phases which exist everywhere, and which must exist, or action itself cease, and death reign universally.

Growth and eating are antagonistic ; yet, one must eat to live as assuredly as children must be reared at the expense of nutrition, and of still more elaborated parental force. Nor is it true that one who expends least has the most remaining. Other things being equal, the law seems to be directly reversed. One activity initiates another ; the largest individual force maintains those more active adjustments, " simultaneous and successive," between the internal and external, which indicate the most vigorous life. We must look, then, to something more than a direct antagonism, between growth and reproduction, to account for unlikenesses of the sexes in plant or animal.

Mr. Spencer reasons that birds, as a class, are less in size than mammals, because they habitually expend more muscular energy in flight ; and that lions having a digestive system not superior to men, yet attain to a larger size and are more prolific, because they have a less active nervous system to sustain. Then, if women normally have equal appropriative powers with men, the surplus nutriment not needed for their smaller *physiques* may be constitutionally handed over to reproduction. Natural selection has originated an admirably complete system of related provisions to this distinct end. This fact must lead us to the conclusion that the aggregate of feminine force is the full and fair equivalent of all masculine force physical or psychical.

The maternal constitution elaborates nutriment from which it is itself to receive no direct benefit But do we forget the inexorable conditions which compel the human father to expend equivalent muscular or mental force to feed, not himself, but his dependents ? Whenever man does not interfere monogamy seems to be the general order of Nature with all higher organisms. Where the cost of obtaining food is great, the parents sustain commensurate burdens in rearing their young; and, with these claims, I think it will be found that monogamy is the primal condition of reproduction. The warlike duty of defence is also borne chiefly by males, and must often be an immense tax on the energies.

Among the beings of a lower type, plant and animal, all the more recent observations indicate that Nature herself systematically favors the females—the mothers of the destined races. Nature's sturdiest buds and her best-fed butterflies belong to this sex ; her female spiders are large enough to eat up a score of her little males ; some of her mother-fishes might parody the nursery-song, "I have a little husband no bigger than my thumb." Natural selection, whether the working out of intelligent design or otherwise, would make this result inevitable. We might expect that the neuter bee could be nourished into the queen-mother. If required to judge *à priori*, we should decide, if there is no predetermination of sex, that the best-fed embryos would most readily become female ; since the one special fact in the feminine organism is the innate tendency to manufacture, and, within certain limits, to store up reserved force for the future needs of offspring.

In women, if there is a greater arrest of individual growth than in men, the difference begins in the fœtal life ; their comparative weight and size at birth are the same as at maturity ; and, if the former finish their growth earlier, it must be because relatively they grow more rapidly. The feminine circulation and respiration are both quicker ; and so are the female mental processes. When the whole subject has been quantitatively investigated with sufficient exactness, I believe it will be found that, what man has gained in "massiveness," woman has gained in rapidity of action ; and that all their powers of body and mind, *mathematically computed*, are, and will continue to be, real and true equivalents. The premises are already sufficiently known to compel me to this conclusion.

One point more. Physical and psychical growth in man are not arrested simultaneously. After the body has ceased to grow, the brain-system still enlarging and compacting its highly-mobile structure, mental power increases long after the more rigid, merely mechanical forces have reached their maximum. The same law applies, at least, in equal degrees to woman. If there is any proof that feminine psychical powers normally reach an earlier cessation of growth than the masculine, then, so far as I can learn, no scientist has yet collated the facts and put them before the world in evidence. On the contrary, so far is the earlier physical maturity of woman from necessitating a corresponding earlier psychical maturity, that, in the light of physiological relations, we may deduce the exactly opposite hypothesis.

In woman, maximum mental power should be reached at a considerably later period than in man, because the greater cost of reproduction, though related chiefly to the physical economy, is indirectly psychical; tending to diminish intellectual action also, and to retard its evolution. The cost of all reproductive provisions fully met, and the child-bearing age at an end, the special constitutional tendency to accumulate reserve force will not be immediately destroyed. Functions, active hitherto in the interest of posterity, go on now to accumulate in the interest of the individual. Still further, the naturally less overtaxed intellectual faculties of woman now have *this* advantage also over those of man—an advantage as least as great as the previous disadvantage.

When the vast weight of past social conditions is considered, that women thus far have failed to acquire large powers of abstract thinking and feeling, affords no reason for supposing that there is a corresponding constitutional lack of ability in this direction. They attain an earlier growth, but, that they reach the highest point even of physical vigor earlier than men, we have no evidence. Many facts indicate otherwise. Men and women live to equal ages, retain their vigor to equal ages — those using the greater force more slowly, these the lesser force more rapidly—thus with uneven steps keeping even pace in physical progress ; the greater mobility of all womanly functions being less readily stiffened into inactivity. This principle, applied to the nervous system, should prolong the period of greatest mental activity, and hold the balance which measures the working value of the sexes with even justice.

Is it true that average women to-day are less versed than average men in abstract thinking, feeling, or acting ?   Not in New England !   Not in any locality where they have equal education. They have not become *savants!* But circumstances have not yet impelled them to become such. In these days, philosophers grow by steady accretions, like every thing else. No full-armed Minerva can be expected to spring by simple heredity from a paternal Jupiter ; but the laws of mental inheritance are too little known to enable us to decide that the daughters of the nineteenth century are less gifted than the sons. When women are convinced that the antagonisms between growth and reproduction, though embracing all personalities, must yet leave them all intact, every thing else may be left to adjust itself, with no solicitude for the ultimate results.

SEX AND WORK.

I.

Dr. E. H. Clarke's timely book on "Sex in Education," seems to me to be the result of earnestness, observation, and humane thought; and yet it is so hopelessly one-sided that there is no choice left to women except to hold up the subject afresh in other points of view. His suggestions, largely practical, laying down a distinct line of conduct for schools and colleges, and bearing authoritatively upon one of the most practical questions of the day—that of continuing and enlarging the existing system of co-education of the sexes—are all suggestions drawn " solely from the stand-point of physiology."

But this is not a question of physiology merely. Whatever view we may take of the nature of body

and mind, yet it is certain that school education is
psychical rather than physical, that mental influences
are as potent in maintaining the health of the body,
and are as intimately associated in the regulation of
all its functions, as these same bodily functions are in
influencing the character and strength of mental
activities. Physiology is not competent to sit in
judgment alone upon this question. The regimen
suggested might directly strengthen and build up the
feminine mechanism ; but the mental and moral
influences reacting would pull it down again fourfold.
A recurring idleness to be grafted upon our scheme
of school education ; potent to foster the thought and
the weaknesses of invalidism, and left free to nurture
hurtful revery and growing sexual sentiment, at all
the most critical periods of the most sensitive years of
young maidenhood, would be infinitely pernicious.
The evils would overbalance even the good of robust
health ; but robust health would be impossible under
such conditions. Better the present school system of
overwork—perpetual and unremitted overwork, both
for girls and boys—mischievous as this is, with its
long train of yet untold horrors. Even the murder

of the innocents is not the worst evil which might befall them !

I have a sincere appreciation of the excellent service done in calling attention seriously to the more complex, more highly organized, and, therefore, more readily imperilled feminine organism with its added rythmical complexity of functions, which cannot be too carefully or continuously guarded from disturbance. Every possible provision of sound physiological common sense should undoubtedly be made in the whole structure of society for protecting the health of its women. School girls should be guarded from injurious educational systems as the apple of the nation's eye, and early taught to understand that, even more than boys, they are are fearfully and wonderfully made ; requiring, therefore, to use a higher discretion in maintaining equally robust health.

If this discussion should teach women to honor and reverence the natures which God has given them ; if it should teach men that there is an eternal basis for the chivalry, the courtesy, with which they are wont to treat women—for which graceful attentions our own countrymen are especially distinguished—

if it should teach even the rudest boyhood some dis-
cernment of the respect and tenderness which are
justly due to their sisters, then women may easily
more than forgive Dr. Clarke for his somewhat
obtuse perception of the nature of their justly and
readily wounded sensibilities. They can afford to
receive with magnanimity his unjust assertion as to
the tendency of " the new gospel of female development," and to forget his unlovely pictures of an impossible, unsexed womanhood.

But when Dr. Clarke characterizes masculine methods of study and work by " persistency," and feminine methods by " periodicity," he can have no really
scientific basis for such a distinction. Strictly persistent study is a human impossibility. Every student
must eat at least one or two meals a day—three are
not usually supposed to be too many—and must
require time and rest for the furtherance of a good
digestion. Then there is the added periodicity of
sleep, recurring every twenty-four hours; one of nature's many beautiful, rythmical adjustments which
abound in endless and admirable variety in all things
animate and inanimate. Every action in Nature is

rythmical, and all human functions are naturally adjusted to nature's methods. Then why is the school girl to be singled out from all humanity and condemned to whole days under the cruel tuition of idleness? Any healthful school regimen, which will enable a boy to develop his larger muscles and brain, and his special organism, must be one which will allow a girl of the same age to develop her lesser muscles and brain and her more complex organism, with equal facility and robustness.

How many hours of daily study should be imposed on a growing boy of sixteen? Let Science settle that question and then assign to the girl of sixteen the same lessons and require the same average scholarship. She will need fewer hours of study than he; for the mental processes of the average girl are as much more rapid than the boys, as her physical growth and development is in advance of his, and we may safely leave it to her feminine tact and common sense to study when she is quite able to do so and not otherwise. When girls of sixteen are to be classed with boys of eighteen or twenty, and expected to keep even steps, as now generally happens in schools of a higher grade for both sexes, here is an injustice, a positive oppression, sustained by false and exacting public sentiment. This we do well to remedy. But if we are to foster and cultivate habits of immeasurable dawdle, mental and physical, in all our school girls, and are expected to transplant Dr. Clarke's system of girl-culture into our homes, we shall soon become a nation of hypochondriacs.

II.

Sensible, good little German maidens, "physically very strong," may be content to remain prisoners for days in their own rooms, in a lamb-like quietude of mood, with no quickening of inspiration towards mischief and merry-making, or of aspiration towards a more serious utilizing of brain-power. It is difficult to disprove the good results of time-honored usages in refined, orderly communities, which stand out prominently as wholesome examples to our cruder types of society. But these model girls must be the aristocratic cousins of the famous Hans;

the dutiful son who carried his grist to mill on horse-back, balanced by a stone, because "fadder did so, and grandfadder did so."

Our girls see more of that variety of women from the Old World who are able to work three hundred and sixty-five days every year in the New, and still maintain vigorous health ; they have concluded, there-fore, to strike a happy average between the two extremes of the European regimen. It suits our democratic institutions better ; allowing all the girls to profit by our national system of schools, and all of them to learn to work, also, if they are so minded. Why not ?

The American development of nerves and of con-sequent ill health, has a much deeper and broader root than the common school system of joint educa-tion. It is grounded in all our methods of business occupation, male and female. Every physician does well to make a stand against it, to lift up his voice in solemn warning against every influence which is likely to increase the growing evil. But why single out the poor little school-girl-class, between thirteen and twenty, as the one group above all others from which to draw the most impressive moral? There are tens of thousands, both of American and foreign-born maidens, also in their teens, who have left school, who are toiling in country homes and in city work-shops, having no day of rest except Sunday, and not always that. Are they stronger in physique than the others—the more favored class? Is physical toil less trying to the feminine constitution than moderate daily study? No; rather more so.

At the late World's Exposition in Vienna, Europe begged of America to give her recipe for quickening the mental activity of the working classes. But we couldn't give it. We don't know what it is ourselves. This world-renowned quickening of the clods from the very feet upwards, which is patent enough to all, is a spontaneous self-growth; no one is especially responsible for the process which produces it. But whatever promotes its growth, influences women and young girls, home-bred and imported, equally with all other classes. The recklessness and self-confidence with which we entered into the conduct of our share in that very Exposition is a very fair illustration of the "people's methods," with their frequent mortifying failures and equally frequent but more gratifying successes. Whether good or bad, our national modes of work are a natural outgrowth from our peculiar social conditions. They influence women, and their methods of study, and work, and recreation, more powerfully perhaps than men ; and young girls, from the national latitude and freedom of manners, more than any other class, not excepting male young America.

Any improved regimen, to be successful, must be somewhere in line with the old, which Dr. Clarke's certainly is not. The majority of quite young girls would probably rejoice in an established reprieve from study ; and would cheerfully entertain themselves on their sofas in the free enjoyment of gossiping, novel-reading, hurtful aimless day dreaming, or sentimental composition in prose or poetry ; all tending to make healthful study, for a time, a simple impossibility. It would be equivalent to the direct nurture of every incipient tendency to coquetry, indolence, selfishness, castle-building, aimlessness, childishness, hysteria, and all manner of fancied or real invalidism. An active mind cannot rest indefinitely.

Teach it to work easily, healthfully, not too continuously, and all must be well. But persistently thwart its normal exercise, and many nameless evils will be the result.

It seems superfluous and humiliating to continue this line of argument; but the grave possibility that the "regimen of intermittence" may be practically adopted by a single school in all the land, gives me courage to proceed.

Would the most unreckoning adviser as to a fit system of education for boyhood, at the critical age of early puberty, counsel the shutting him up in a room for days together, without occupation, either alone or in the presence of young companions? Yet the danger could be little less perilous for girlhood. She might be less liable to be driven to outward vice; but the evil of fostering a depraved or weak sentimentality would be fearfully imminent. Women, from their past education, are already infirm enough in purpose, narrow enough in aims, and low enough in aspirations. The proposed system of training would multiply these evils fourfold. Far be it from me to suggest that there is any unusual tendency to evil-mindedness in our innocent young girls, whose brightness, beauty, and frank fearlessness are a guarantee for their womanly integrity. But if our educated young women were to be required habitually to wrench their minds free from books and wholesome improvement, they would assuredly . fix them upon less profitable subjects of interest.

And why resort to separate school systems for boys and girls ? Daily, habitual, moderate exercise is as desirable and wholesome for a healthy girl as for any other human being ; and some daily brain-work is equally indispensable for the strength and harmony of her development.

It is not true that the womanly organism perfects itself by spasmodic, rhythmical jerks of growth and advancement. It is more or less active, but never torpid ; as the stomach is stimulated to activity by an ample supply of food to digest, though its processes are never entirely passive. This is true of all bodily functions.

Deciduous trees perform a large amount of work even in winter. They look desolate, lifeless ; yet, in the midst of their covering of ice and snow, their slow activity is steadily nurturing every bud and fibre of the whole plant. February finds all growth much farther advanced than December. When the sap begins to circulate freely in the vegetable veins, the tree is ready to burst into sudden greenness and blossoms. If Nature can accomplish thus much out in the cold, she ought to be able steadily to mature her young women in harmonious strength and vigor amid the warmth and comfort of well-regulated homes and school rooms. She asks only that we co-work with her intelligently, instead of directly counteracting her processes. When she is most active in carrying forward her nutritive processes, then is the time for us to be most restful and least exacting in the use both of brain and muscle. A wise poet will not habitually choose the few hours subsequent to a banquet for verse-making, unless he has imbibed too freely of stimulating beverages ; and any school girl of fair ability, if not over-stimulated by her instructors, can maintain a standing in her class equal to that of boys of her own age, and yet leave all her womanly functions quite unimpaired. Let her be physiologically instructed ; but do let us rely on her feminine good sense to adapt her methods of work to her own special constitutional needs.

Who can be certain, if ever so well versed in anatomy, physiology, and pathology, that nature is required to be more rigorous in her exactions of a young woman than of a little girl? Which of us, by taking thought, can add one more cell to the growing organism? A good digestion will guarantee a well-balanced physical development. The child is endlessly in motion, exercising every muscle the most completely just when all its tissues are forming most rapidly. It wastes material recklessly, but the waste stimulates repair ; the use strengthens the used member and all the correlated functions of the entire organism.

On the same principle let every girl exercise mind and body fearlessly, with wholesome vigor and in due proportion. She is not porcelain to be easily broken, nor are the adjustments of her nature so weakly put together that they can be readily disturbed, or so fearfully balanced that the slightest overwork in one direction must mean weakness or disease in some other as penalty.

III.

Probably there are few women who do not instinctively shrink from a popular discussion of the
influence of sex in the affairs of life—not that nature's methods are ever gross or indelicate, but because public sentiment has so often shown itself to
be ignorantly and wickedly perverted. But the time
evidently has come for putting aside hesitation and
steadily meeting the whole range of considerations
which the community are determined shall be pressed
home to all who advocate enlarged culture and a
wider sphere of activities for women. The discussion will be timely, and it should be of immense practical value ; since it is now very generally conceded
that it is not so much the work to be done as the
methods of working, which will hereafter practically
determine the sphere of the two sexes.

Dr. Clarke has given voice and tangibility to
many of the floating suggestions of years, insisting
that women are physically incapacitated for habitual
study, that growing young girls should not be allowed

to compete with boys in an identical course of education, and leading us squarely up to the inference that the strain of persistent mental work can never be successfully borne by average womanhood. The Dr. pronounces our national, rapidly growing method of co-education in schools and colleges "a crime before God and humanity, that physiology protests against, and that experience weeps over." The entire community, therefore, has a most vital interest in this book, which maintains that co-education is more than a mistake; that it imperils the health of the girls, curtailing their hope of posterity, and threatening their few possible children with greatly enfeebled constitutions.

But women must be more competent witnesses than any man can be. The fact that they are coming forward at all points to take part in the discussion, shows their instinctive, their mutually helpful recognition of this truth. Many of us have felt for years that the "Woman question" must be met just here, upon a comparative physiological and psychological basis; yet we have hesitated and waited till, thanks to Dr. Clarke, to hold back now would be a tacit acknowledgment of the correctness of his conclusions.

His statement as to certain leading traits of feminine structure and functions seems to me clearer and broader than can be found in standard works, and to have gone beyond any of the old physiologies in a just comprehension of nature's divergent methods in her endowments of men and women. One may frankly accept both his physical and his psychical main premises, and may do him justice as having planted himself upon a basis high enough to admit the theory of Woman's equality, and yet differ from him at every turn in a practical direction.

The every-day question is, does study, a few hours of regular daily application to mental work, impair or tend to impair the vigor of the feminine constitution? Are the daily lessons which are fitting and healthful for a school boy so exacting that they must draw the blood to nurture the brain of the school girl to the detriment of her appropriate womanly growth? Does moderate study, on any day and at any period of a healthy woman's life, tend to exhaust her natural strength, or to produce a reaction so violent that it must become a direct promoter either of weakness or of disease? These questions are all one ; they apply to the girl of fifteen or to the woman of thirty alike. They must be answered as bearing not only on her own welfare, but also on that of the rising generation.

There are many ways of reaching the same conclusion, but the first and best method is based upon experience. Col. Higginson, like many others, is collecting data upon this point. He pertinently insists that we must determine whether the girls who have received a co-education with young men, or any other similar education, are less healthy than their more unlearned sisters. It is fitting that I add personal testimony to enforce my position, that study is as healthful to women as to men, and, as society now is, that it must prove to be relatively much more so.

In the days when mothers sent their babies for early instruction, I was a little school-girl in prompt and regular attendance at three years. I remained at school, averaging from a half to two-thirds of every intervening year, until I was twenty-four ; so that I have literally "come of age" under a system of joint

education for the sexes, for I never attended a girls'
school. During this whole period I studied as continuously as an average boy studies, was not conspic-
uously deficient at recitations, and for years together
did more real brain work outside of all class exercises
than in connection with them; yet my health was
generally good, and it continued good for years after
I left the Theological Seminary, though I was engaged in work more health-trying than anything in
my previous experience. Once, not from ordinary
overwork, but in passing through an ordeal not un-
common in modern days, in which the faith of one's
fathers is shaken to the foundations, and when forced
to meet the added struggle of continuing to teach
many things which were no longer believed, or dropping out from a profession chosen conscientiously in
the face of untold obstacles, my health was seriously
impaired. But I speedily gained both a broader faith
and a firmer health, which remain unimpaired to this
day. I am the mother of six children, five of whom
enjoy a vigor of constitution above the average ; and
one, in the midst of apparently perfect health, was
swept off by one of those scourges of infancy against

which Omniscience alone could always guard effect-ively. During my married life I have averaged cer-tainly three hours of daily habitual brain work, not including daily papers and miscellaneous light read-ing. By a whimsical coincidence, this period has covered just eighteen years ; so that I have reached " the legal age for a woman " in matrimony.

Perhaps one may be pardoned for adding that, though quite awake to the many casualties which may shorten life, I am confidently looking forward to twenty-five or thirty, or even more than forty, years yet of vigorous working powers. This I have a fair right to anticipate, as the daughter of a mother who lived to be more than eighty, and a father whose still active mind in his now worn body will reach ninety-one on his approaching birth-day.

We may regard this as an exceptional instance of a woman's ability to endure persistent brain work un-harmed in health ; but I believe it to be simply one illustration of human power to thrive on habitual daily exercise of both mind and body, alternated with sufficient rest and relaxation.

We require many similar facts before we can decide this question solely from the basis of experience. Meantime the apparent physical strength of such women as Mrs. Somerville, who lived to .write science and philosophy at ninety years, is at least encouraging. Among living women there are Miss Martineau, Frances Power Cobb, and many other robust women of eminent mental attainments in England. In America, Mrs. Child, Catherine Beecher, Miss Cushman, Prof. Maria Mitchell, Drs. Elizabeth and Emily Blackwell, Mary L. Booth, Grace Greenwood, and the host of women who have done the largest share of brain work in every direction for a quarter of a century past, the majority of them have health much above the standard rates. They lead us to hope that, if they would condescend to give in their "Woman's testimony" according to good old-fashioned Quaker precedent, they would generally agree substantially in the opinion that reasonable brain work habitually performed can have no inherent tendency to undermine the feminine constitution.

IV.

Statistics in the interest of a theory are said to be proverbially unreliable ; but it needs only the most casual observation to convince any impartial mind that four-fifths of those among our country women who, for years past, have been most active in any branch of work, from the lowest to the highest, are the women who have had the most reliable health, who have been most uniformly exempt from chronic feebleness, and from frequent severe illness. Among this active class we shall find the nearest approximation to really vigorous constitutions, such as would honor any nationality and any conditions, the most favorable to feminine well-being.

One has only to look among his own acquaintances in town and country to verify this assertion. Let him compare the wives, who habitually do some of their own house work, with others, who are simply ladies of leisure. Let him take note of the women who have been most active in benevolent enterprises in his locality, or who sustained the Sanitary Com-

mission and similar charities during the war; of the
business women who conduct thread and needle
stores and kindred industries; of the teachers, the
writers, the lecturers, the artists, and of all the active
leaders and managers in every rank of society. Compare any of these with idlers whose general methods
of living in other respects are most similar. Or, compare the working girls in homes and factories with
the dainty misses who live on tid-bits! Who have
nerves and headaches? Who have feminine weaknesses? Who have ailments more than the stars of
heaven for number? Not the servant girl, but her
"little mistress;" not the most active women, but
the most inactive.

The great cry which has been raised of late years
over the failing health of American women may turn
out to have been fully one-half panic. So long as the
most fascinating of their sex luxuriate in a superior
delicacy of constitution, and plume themselves upon
their extra fragility as beautiful and interesting, their
physicians and the sensitive gentlemen of the press,
whose business it is to chronicle the status of the
"society" to which they are allied, must naturally

look at the feminine world through the glamor of this
rose-colored invalidism. A wider outlook may partially reverse the picture. It is one of my firmest
convictions that if overwork has slain its thousands
of women, underwork has slain its tens of thousands,
who have perished more miserably. Dr. Brown-
Séquard assures us that both men and beasts in this
country have a greater tenacity of life and more prolonged endurance than among European nations. So
great is this difference, he says, that when our physiologists make plain statements of fact which have some
bearing upon this point, the *savans* of Europe believe
them guilty of exaggeration and of serious untrust-
worthiness. Let our physicians, preachers, lecturers,
and journalists, then, look at the situation afresh in
the light of Dr. Brown-Séquard's most authoritative
assertion. We may find that the home type of
womanhood, something less in avoirdupois, is something more in endurance than the trans-Atlantic
variety ; and that Nature has contrived to maintain
her balance of values here as elsewhere.

The reason for this superior tenacity of life, as
the Doctor thinks, lies in the diminished tendency to

hemorrhage. So great is the difference in this respect that a rabbit, upon which he performed an operation, so severe that the creature might be expected to die under his hands if in Europe, in New York was able to go on quietly eating away at a carrot—let us hope, enjoying the equanimity of a comforting instinctive philosophy. Is there a corresponding difference of functional tendencies on the opposite sides of the ocean? This might enable our women to pursue their ordinary occupations at all times with less inconvenience than abroad, and with diminished danger to health. It is a question worth considering, one which can be best answered, perhaps, by our adopted country women. Multitudes, American-born, are ready to insist that if any moderate exercise, a few hours of study, or the excitements of an ordinary recitation, are sufficient at any period to produce exhausting and abnormal hemorrhage, that this fact is in itself sufficient evidence of health already so much impaired as to require the treatment adapted to invalids. It must be safe to conclude that habits, which have grown up unnoticed and without concerted action in all grades of a community, have something to recommend them beyond the perversity of sheer caprice. By all means, then, let our *savans* reconsider the feminine health question from a fresh climatic standpoint.

It is profitable to consult other countries and older times; but no customs, no system of regulations, except the simple moral law, can have binding force in extremely unlike conditions. Levitical law, needful and perhaps imperative in a nomadic age, when the whole nation was weary and footsore with toilsome marches, would be as inappropriate for the petted parlor women of to-day as typical sacrifices and ceremonial customs for our religious observance.

Health, and working-force, rise and fall together. Dr. Clarke's opponents have insisted that the best students are also the healthiest girls; his defenders answer that because they are healthy they can become good students. Both are right. Health promotes study; and the converse is also true; study promotes health. The use of faculty develops it; function brought into exercise is function strengthened and toned to new vigor. Work is health-giving, of constitutional necessity. We may safely challenge disproof of this assertion ; for the principle is as deep and as broad as the foundations of all organic nature.

To promote digestion we must supply not merely food to digest ; but a body active enough to assimilate nutriment. A weak system is often surfeited and its action clogged, with more nourishment than it knows how to utilize. Many a dyspeptic girl could comfortably digest twice the amount of food which she now does sufferingly, if she had either brain or muscles energetic enough to require the product of digestion for the renewal of their rapidly expended tissues. Loss of appetite and general feebleness are another consequence of excessive inactivity.

Every stroke of the blacksmith's hammer is equal to knocking out an equivalent amount of muscle from his own arm. But the life forces rush to the breach ; they throw aside the debris ; crowd in fresh material more compactly than before, in repairing the waste; and thus they persistently enlarge and strengthen the whole structure to an iron-like endurance. The more active the loss, the more energetic the repair ; and the more powerful becomes the living tissue which thus has been wrought and re-wrought into massive strength.

Whether this process of active waste and renewal is carried forward in the arms, or in the brain, the result is identical. Added size, compactness, and more convolutions in the physical brain, represent material nutriment and the added power which it confers. Vigorous use of any faculty means rapidity of circulation, or its equivalent in strength of circulation—means a vital activity inaugurated in the used member, but communicated and distributed in some measure to the whole body. That brain work, in this respect, is less healthful or less influential for good to the general system, than ordinary physical exercise, it would be difficult to prove ; at any rate the burden of proof lies with those who assert that it is so. It is more rapid in its processes, and therefore more quickly exhausting; but I am prepared to hazard the unqualified statement that, independent of added mental and moral influences which are immeasurable —where the existing body of facts are physiologically interpreted, and admitted principles are scientifically applied—it will be found that the habitual exercise of brain-force is as invigorating, physically, as is that of any other class of activities.

V.

The nervous system is the brain system of the body, the mechanism especially adapted to all processes of thought, of feeling, of voluntary motion; to all those reflex activities, which simulate voluntary movement, and to the promotion of all the organic processes of growth and nutrition. Nerves are literally the brain extended; ramified into every minutest part of the body; accompanying the blood vessels everywhere; branching into every muscle, and impelling the entire system to activity. They are formed of the identical peculiar white and gray matter of the brain, every fibre closely modelled after a uniform pattern of growth; as every twig, branch, trunk and root in an ordinary tree is one in structure.

Like arteries and veins, the nerves branch outwards from their centres to every toe and finger tip, and return again in distinct lines. The heart is the recognized great organ of the wonderful branching tree of hollow tubes, in which the blood of the system circulates; and the brain, of the even more marvellous and vital banyan-tree of nerves, which establishes its partially independent ganglia, or new roots at all the important centres where they are needed to carry forward the endlessly complicated processes of active life.

Nerves have long been recognized as having special feminine relations.

How incredibly singular, blind, and perverse, then, is the dogmatism which has insisted that man's larger brain, measured by inches in the cranium, must necessarily prove his mental superiority to Woman. First, let Dr. Brown-Séquard, or some other learned professor of the rapidly growing science of the nervous system, demonstrate the special significance of the unique feminine plexus of nerves in the mammary glands, as related to the emotional, intuitional and moral nature of womanhood. Let us comprehend something more of the supplemental nerves which grow, and live, and die, in the new uterus ; which itself grows, and acts, and lives, and dies in the interest, not of the mother but of her unborn babe ; yet which also profoundly influences her life, physical and psychical. Let us distinctly understand how the feminine brain-system, with all its adjuncts, differs from the masculine ; then, if the facts warrant the conclusion, let man's old-time claim to superiority be vaunted with equal confidence, but on the basis of a more enlightened understanding.

When we learn to balance mass of tissue, strength of action, amount or quantity in all its forms of being and doing in Man, against the more complex structure and the more rapid action of corresponding functions in Woman, we may conclude that the predominating greater velocity is a fair offset to the greater power. The more complex feminine structure, since it is entirely complete within a considerably smaller model, must be proportionately more delicate in workmanship ; this may involve finer tissues and subtler processes throughout, and these may represent equivalent forces. The suggestion is credible.

All physiologists teach us that the feminine skin is thinner and more active, the circulation quicker, and the respiration more frequent ; all satirists affirm that Woman's nerves have a sharper edge ; it is orthodox to believe that her feelings are more acute, and her intuitions more rapid. What hinders, then, the conclusion that what man has "gained in power," he has "lost in velocity?" Or, reverse the law. What Woman has "gained in velocity," she has "lost in power." Who is prepared to show that they are not started in life as equals, on an identical plane of evolution?

It is hazardous to rely altogether upon an *à priori* dogmatism, learned or unlearned, which forces one to set up the assumption that the Creator has been driven by partiality to model an unbalanced, unsymmetrical humanity; like an unshapely apple, one half large and desirable, but the other half small and unsavory.

No want of symmetry is involved, if we accept the theory of variety in equivalents. Regarded as peers, equals in all the qualities of force, physical, mental, and moral, the creative fatherhood is vindicated, and Woman ennobled; but Man not degraded. The *à priori* argument, to me, is completely reversed. Omnipotence might create one vessel to honor, and another to dishonor; but Benificence would be obliged to look far before it could find an adequate motive in that direction.

How the few really great men of the world reach
out to shake hands with each other, across an ocean
or a continent, more rejoiced at a word from one of
these, an equal, than with endless plaudits from the
millions of inferiors ! The appreciation and companionship of one's equals is everywhere the social element of highest value. Add to this the responsive,
quickening influences, which react with special enthusiasm between the sexes, and you have my highest
ideal of the sustaining and thoroughly ennobling
effects which arise from human sympathy. But Man,
forever bowing his royal head, craning his moral neck,
and dropping his eyes from their heavenward outlook
down to Woman, is not an edifying social arrange-
ment, nor can it be a pleasant means of grace to either
party.

Even if Nature's creative forces be regarded as
acting blindly, without moral forecast, yet what sufficient reason can we assign for supposing the sexes, so
equally balanced numerically, to be so unequally
balanced in all highest values ? Fortunately, it is a
question to be ultimately decided on the comparative
evidence of nerve and muscle, and their quality and

quantity of functions ; on the balanced testimony of thought and feeling, of logic and intuition and similar equivalent forces. " The old man and his deeds" decreed himself the superior ; the new woman by her deeds is asserting her equality ; now on which side will Nature declare herself, if scientifically interrogated ?

At present we are inquiring only as to the capacity of the sexes to perform equivalent amounts of work uninjured. Man can lift a heavier weight ; but woman can watch more enduringly at the bedside of her sick child. Such at least is the current belief ; and if physiology can show us that the added periodicity of function in her constitution, intimately connected as it is with the circulation of the blood in every artery and vein, must confer on her an added impulse towards the perpetual renewal of exhausted health, through this surplus method of eliminating worn tissues and relieving over-taxed nerves, here is one point gained. That such is the result, every woman and every physician must testify. Whenever her work is endurance, whenever patient waiting and some degree of enforced muscular and mental inactivity is necessitated by her maternal functions, before and after the birth of children, then extraordinary organic processes re-establish the balance. Nature, by unlike but kindred methods, has instituted a special system of provisions for the preservation and renewal of the health of woman. These provisions are adapted alike to overwork and to underwork ; as the evil arising in either case is a disturbed action to the whole system. They are as admirably adjusted to the over use of the intellectual and emotional faculties as to excessive muscular activity. They are special provisions, related not simply to maternal functions, but are needed, also, by the generally more rapid activity of the more excitable feminine temperament.

My conclusion, therefore, is that an equivalent amount of work, mental or physical, though it will be performed in somewhat different ways by men and women, other things being equal, could often be borne more successfully by the average woman than by the average man.

VI.

The "irrepressible woman question" is broader and more radical in every direction than most of us have been accustomed to think. No one can read the discussion now going forward in this country and England—some of it called to the surface just now by the educational question, but more of it beginning immensely lower down in the heavy scientific strata which underlie all questions of social life and progress —without comprehending that Woman and her cause are rapidly coming to the front. They rise up in new and unhoped-for relations, which must arouse the thinking world to an early consideration of our long, persistently reiterated Bill of Rights.

One can only hope that women themselves will prove equal to the occasions—ready not only to step into the openings which are made for them ; but to stand there steadily as pillars of strength and competence. But to doubt this, would be heresy ! No one can know how strong women really are, until they can find a chance to measure their work with commensurate masculine achievements. This they have not been able to do in the past. The world has insisted, and still insists, whenever it attempts an estimate, on measuring the woman's work directly by the man's standards. If it falls short according to these, it is allowed no other appreciable merit. Theological and logical theories, alike, teach that Man is physically and mentally the greater, Woman the less ; he the Ordained or the Evolved superior, she the Heaven-appointed or the Natural-selection-produced inferior. Her work falls below his, both in quantity and quality ; but it has nothing of difference, or of unlikeness, worth noting—at least, nothing beyond the reproductive functions common to the whole race of mammals.

But the scientists have proved that heat enough to warm one pound of water one degree in temperature, is exactly as great as the mechanical power needed to move seven hundred and seventy-two pounds of water one foot up-hill. They have calculated that "the magnitude of the chemical force of attraction between the particles of a pound of coal, and the quantity of oxygen that corresponds to it, is capable of lifting a weight of one hundred pounds to a height of twenty miles."

This is estimating unlike modes of power in terms of common value. It appears that a small fraction of heat is equal to a large amount of lifting power—that the energy locked up in a single pound of coal, rightly utilized, can do more positive work than the muscles of ten thousand stalwart giants. One would suppose, then, however great the difficulty of accurately measuring the differing modes of energy in men and women respectively, that scientific men might suspect the possibility of some natural adjustment and equivalence of value in the two sexes! But if they do, we find no evidence of it in their latest conclusions. On the contrary, they are now scientifically remanding Woman to a position of permanent mental inferiority.

Is it not quite time, then, for woman to reconsider the ground work of these conclusions, if possibly the *savants* have furnished and pointed the weapons which can be effectually used for the overthrow of such grossly one-sided theories? Size and strength are not always indicative of the greater power; and we shall certainly find that men and women differ, not so much in the degrees of ability which they manifest, as in the different modes in which they expend their energies, physical and mental. Their work is as generically unlike as the effects of heat, of lifting force, of chemical affinity, or of any other of the recognized modes of material energy. If each is to be justly estimated in comparison, they must each first receive a just estimate in his and her own right.

It is possible, also, that both sexes might be greatly benefited, if they could learn to convert some of the surplus lower modes of energy into the higher, thus securing a better balance of development individually, and promoting nobler social results.

Revised physiology affirms that habitual study must overtax the health of growing girls. But it is notorious that girls ordinarily suffer, not from too much thought, but from over-stimulated and mis-directed feeling. Women generally have either too many nerves or too little nerve-force to maintain the balance and keep the nerves always in pleasant working order. The majority of boys and men, on their side, are neither too intellectual nor too largely developed in self-control. Then what class of energies could be most profitably converted into dominant nerve-force and power of the higher varieties? Not thought, but feeling ; sentiment or sense-influences in some of their many phrases—varying in character with the age, the sex, and the personal temperament.

A diet of novel-reading, a social course of early flirtation, of juvenile party-going, and similar fashionable methods of promoting a precocious interest in the opposite sex, tend also to anticipate the age of puberty. Similar causes unduly tax the sexual functions at all ages. Emotion of every kind, even the most refined and loftiest types, if not carried forward into adapted modes of action, tend to the same results. Few children can be disproportionately cultivated in musical talent, or in any form of emotional or artistic development, and not reach a precocious manhood or womanhood. The little servant girl, with her habits simple and robust, remains child-like much longer than her "little mistress," who becomes enfeebled in proportion. Even a religious zeal, which cultivates devotional feeling as an end, rather than as a force to impel to religious deeds, is necessarily, constitutionally a direct promoter of weak health or of real immorality.

The Divine Order, evidently, never intended that men or women should live chiefly in the feelings ; and His penalties are handed down to the third and fourth generations ! The special failings and temptations of the sexes are unlike; often as remote as the East is from the West; but whichever persists in the special culture of sentiment or sensation, must accept of Nature's established penalties.

But if these are facts, and they will be admitted by physiologists, generally, and may be found stated or indicated in medical journals, then is it credible that daily moderate study, which tends directly to reduce feeling—converting it into an equivalent amount of thought, and judiciously occupying time, attention, and interest—can do more harm than good to even the most delicate class of young girls ? If any thing could give them strength, it would be this relief offered to the monotony of interests, exhausting because of their very persistency. Study is one tonic which they need, but not the only one.

Fretful, nervous, pale-faced women often fritter

away their lives in an endless succession of small
feelings, each good and lovely enough in itself ; but
as the staple of life, the basis of humiliating weakness and real inferiority. With all their faults, men
have either learned to feel less, or else to condense
the amount, with more time for the re-action. Of
course they can work more.

And work is nobler than sentiment—if there is
gradation in the value of equivalent forces. Rather
let us say that faith, hope and love, without works,
are all dead ; and are death-dealing in their influence
upon the possessor.

The future generations would suffer neither in
numbers, nor in health, nor in a general harmony and
elevation of character, if we could promote more sustained intellectual life in connection with a greater
vigor of the whole physical constitution, and less activity of the functions of reproduction. Emotion, in
all its phases, is the proper motive power for the
corresponding activities ; but as an end, in itself, to
man or woman, it is utter destruction.

VII.

A better school discipline, a higher standard of scholarship, improved manners, and even improved morals, are admitted thus far to be some of the direct results of Co-education. The experiment has proved so conclusively that it quickens the minds, refines the manners, and elevates the morals of both sexes, that every doubter now begins by making concessions to this extent ; by way of more effectively calling in question the most complete justification of the experiment in all other respects.

Dr. Clarke is not an exception to this rule. In the face of such admissions, he still speaks of sexual influence in school life, as though it were a matter of grave objection—as though it must be hedged about by a suspicion of evil ; leading in some unexplained way to most serious consequences. To most serious consequences the sexual sentiments do lead inevitably. They are potent forces in school life and in all other life. But with abundant opportunities of studying many educational institutions of all grades,

I never knew of one bad result which could be fairly attributed to Co-education. I have traced many good results, have watched them rising steadily and increasingly ; and have followed them outward into widely different and quite unexpected channels.

Experience and observation should qualify a woman whose life is approaching half a century, half of that life itself a part of the Co-educational system, and the remainder largely devoted to studying its effects, to speak with as much authority on this subject as any one else is likely to do, with only the existing amount of data to observe and reason from. As teacher, my experience has also been miscellaneous enough, and of many varieties—in the Church, in the Sunday School, on the lecture platform, occasional classes ; and, added to these, a term each in two different Public Schools and in two Academies, about one year in all ; but under widely different conditions, admirably adapted to test the merits and demerits of Co-education.

I was " lady principal" in a new, flourishing Academy in Michigan, as it was, with all its Western spirit and versatility, rather more than twenty-eight years ago. Brothers and sisters would come from neighboring towns, furnish rooms, keep house, and attend school. Perhaps a cousin or two, or an acquaintance, would join the domestic club. Yet no scandal arose. The young people had come there to study, and they did study! This proved to be the best possible practical outlet to sentiment. Let any group of both sexes, young or old, become thoroughly interested together in any class of intellectual work— from my noting of facts over and over again, it seems to me as sure as demonstration that this is the best possible safeguard to the morals of the little community. It adds also the pleasantest and highest impetus towards the elevation and utilization of sentiment.

At first, I taught young women chiefly—some of them old enough to feel an elder sisterly sympathy for my first real home-sickness. Small boys were reported to feel, and some of them to say, that they "didn't wish to recite to the schoolma'am." At any rate the Principal offered me a choice of classes; and before the term ended, I was about as likely to be found in the recitation-room, or in the boy's school-room hearing lessons, as in my own proper department.

The result to me was that the task of attending to a recitation, and at the same time keeping a large school in order, was immensely simplified. The outside girls would distress me sometimes by innumerable varieties of mischief. The boys never did. That the pupils gained in the interest which they applied to study, it would be unfair to say. The Principal, by his experience, his good sense, and his genuine enthusiasm, knew how to inspire them in that direction; but it would be safe to say that they lost nothing in school diligence. It is certain that the whole school gained—in the place of a spiritless, home-sick teacher—a live woman who understood thoroughly that she herself was placed on trial, in scholarship, in general competence, and in self-respecting good behavior.

Subsequent to that test, it would be morally impossible to convince me that impulses and fascinations, which exist in all young people as intensely active and mobile sentiments, can not be best managed by enabling them to quicken the higher activities of mind. Emotions perhaps the most powerful of all the sentient forces, we can no longer afford to ignore in any system of education. A complete science of sociology may or may not be ultimately within human attainment; but some progress must be possible in the right practical direction.

The sexual sentiments can be directed, modified, disciplined, or literally transformed into other mental activities. But the young can neither be expected to understand this nor to know how to effect such results. The natural processes tending towards ends so imperatively desirable, must be incorporated in our educational systems. It seems to me that the one course for successful educators to follow with unwavering steadiness, must lie stretched out before them like a direct line of light. It has been repeatedly and abundantly proved that the genial and natural desire of every boy and girl to please the opposite sex, can be made to take the gratifying form of well-learned lessons and courteous behavior. What does this mean, except that here are potent social forces subject to rational influences? Forces which, left to grope blindly and without aid in a sphere of unregu-

lated impulses, are devastating the world ; forces
which, comprehensively directed, in the end would
bring to earth a social millennium

The vanity of self-love, which under the pretense
of cultivating the graces of life and the gracious
courtesies of society, now fashions the innumerable
young prigs of both sexes, can be systematically converted into an intellectual self-respect in the school-
room, better than elsewhere. There, naturally, they
measure more by attainments than by fine clothes or
dainty manners or social position. There, better than
elsewhere, the real immorality of unmeaning flirtation
can be transformed into the morality of bright, genial,
pleasant companionship.

Once I returned to teach for my academical Alma
Mater in a New York town, colonized largely from
New England, and essentially New England in character. The Principal, a dear elderly clergyman, had
tried to mould me after his own heart, to graduate at
Mt. Holyoke Seminary into a chronic teacher or a
missionary. His assistant had been my classmate
from the childhood of both till he started for Dart-
mouth, and I somewhat later, went to Oberlin—

where they admitted women on equal terms, or nearly equal terms, to all departments of study. Half the
pupils had been our former schoolmates. Under
these circumstances, we were not likely to test innova-
tions ; nor was I—given the sole responsibility of the
girls' school-room—to be expected to find the
"governing" part of my duties a sinecure. They
were reasonably good girls, and everybody seemed
satisfied ; but whatever enthusiasm for study I could
awaken in them, they generally saved up to be put
into the lessons which were to be recited "up-stairs."
If they wanted special help, it was often help in pre-
paring the lessons for "up-stairs!" Those same lessons up-stairs! I knew all about them—that they
were generally spirited, well-learned and well-recited.
But the flavor of recitations "down stairs" was often
as insipid as the tepid remnant of soda water left
over in the bottom of the glass.

At Oberlin, where they have a large preparatory
department, at one time I had a class of young ladies
in English Composition. A pleasant and satisfactory
class it was ; yet a similar result was noticeable.
When these young ladies came into classes where

they were expected to read essays in the presence of a professor and gentlemen classmates, the wish to succeed, and the pressing need for assistance or suggestion, were equally manifest.

In a strictly girls' school, of course each would do her best with lessons which needed the most study. And yet, in the mixed school, or in a college like Vassar—which knows that it is to be tested by other colleges, and to be judged in comparison with them—it is certain that the influence which requires an elevated standard of scholarship for the girls, is much less a result from the supposed effect which this will produce upon the opposite sex, than from the steady pressure of the quickened feminine consciousness that every failure now is more than personal failure. The direct influence which most inspires success to every girl comes from her own sex ; the sex which instinctively recognizes that, for the first time in history, it is fairly called on to give proof of its equal intellectual ability.

VIII.

We hear enough of the quickening influence of each sex upon each other in Co-education ; but the special sympathy of women for womanhood, which has been greatly developed in girls in all higher schools, and in women who engage in pursuits unusual to them hitherto, has been but little, if at all, noticed by psychologists. The petty envies and jealousies of women are held up as characteristic of the sex by the surface-seers, whose stock of facts belong chiefly to the mythologies. In the light of existing data, it must be conceded that if there is any characteristic feminine sentiment, it is the specially developed, instinctive *esprit de corps* of woman-hood.

A corresponding sentiment has never been brought equally into exercise in men. But facts will best illustrate the statement.

In schools, the abilities of the girls are tested by those of the boys ; and the girls cannot easily endure failure, either for themselves or for their companions.

This feeling is often strong enough to compel assistance to the more incompetent, and to triumph over even a sense of personal rivalry. The failure of any one is felt, perhaps unconsciously, by all the others, almost as a personal grievance, as a failure which involves the whole sex. Comparatively, a boy may succeed or fail for himself alone. For his confreres, all the ages past are illuminated by examples which cover his deficiencies with their vail of light.

The dull or idle girl feels with certainty that her failures are regarded with much less favor by the girls than by the boys. The boys might continue to admire her still, but the girls would not. Some boys might even regard her incapacity as a special feminine grace ; might plume themselves upon their superior masculine intellects, and return to her the gracious reactionary tribute of their satisfaction. But all the girls must feel that her failures are a shame, almost an insult, to themselves. Thus, they inevitably stimulate each other to success.

Also, the example of one successful girl is more to all the others than any incitement which can come from the superior scholarship of a boy. Emulation is stronger than rivalry. There are felt to be essential differences in the sexes which can never make them the imitators of each other. What men have done, men may do ; yet this will often count for very little to women. But what one woman has achieved, is felt by all the others as a direct quickening example.

Then there is a deep, sisterly sympathy and aid in women for each other ; for which they have never yet received credit. Because society outlawed the wrong-doers of this sex, and set them apart for evil ; so that a respectable woman might not let them touch even the hem of her garment in the older days ; and because the weak and the wicked women were ready to throw stones, as they were induced to do by public opinion, it has come to be believed that women are hard to each other—harder even than men. But this is utterly untrue. No one likes to wear a brand of shame ; and in morals as in intellect, every woman belongs to womanhood as no man can belong to manhood. This is a result, of course, not to be credited to Nature, but to conventionalities. But the effect is the same. The moral failure of one woman is a pain

and humiliation to all ; and this sentiment the masculine judgment has cruelly misconstrued.

But the sympathy of the average woman for all of her
own sex is absolutely unappreciated. The sympathetic
aid which women render each other is not even suspected
by the psychological on-lookers of a sex which has not
been stimulated to develop a corresponding sentiment.

To illustrate. In the Michigan school, to which I
have referred, the Principal, who did nothing by
halves, would sometimes, unexpectedly to me and to
the pupils, desire me to exchange a class with him
for the day. We all understood that this was a test
matter to some of us. The sympathy of the girls
for each other and for me, and mine for them, was
something quite apart from anything we could feel
towards the opposite sex. It was this which made
such ordeals successful as a whole, and which ended
in making them thoroughly gratifying to us all. The
girls stood by me, watchful to help in any emergency,
with a solicitude like that which a family of daughters
might feel for a mother or sister placed in a rather
trying position ; and they were equally loyal to each
other, giving an effective aid from this readily felt

sympathy, unlike in kind, and certainly greater than any male assistance.

It was then and there, also, that I made my first attempt at extemporaneous public speaking. It began with the girls ; but after a few little speeches to them, I took my turn in doing what the Principal was accustomed to do nearly every week. Nominally, I addressed the school ; but the school was gathered in the church, and the whole community invited to attend. In talking to the girls, it was impossible to shake off the feeling that every one of them was able to be coolly critical enough to note each ungrammatical or awkwardly constructed sentence, and to question every doubtful opinion. And so they were. It was not merely feeling ; it was fact.

But in the Church, feminine sympathy was uppermost in every womanly heart. They desired me to succeed, and this spontaneous feeling in their hearts drew off the " stage fright " in mine. This upholding womanly sympathy, I have felt gratefully hundreds of times since, from other audiences. So, consciously or unconsciously, must every woman speaker have done ; especially while public speaking for women

was felt to be a yet untested experiment. Nothing
can prevent the spontaneous womanly aid under such
conditions.

When women first began talking, the conserva-
tive lady, who pinned her faith to a misinterpretation
of St. Paul, sat there, her heart palpitating like all
the others, with one yearning prayer for the fairly
creditable success of the wicked innovator. The
Anti-Woman Suffragists of to-day, can no more see
any woman placed in a position which they feel to
be a trial one to womanhood, and not help her with
the might of an unwilling sympathy, than they
can stop breathing. The success of women in the
earlier days must be largely attributed to this influence.

In the midst of the prejudice, the doubt, the disa-
greeable cavilling and curiosity, feminine sympathy
and the instinct of masculine chivalry rose together.
They were generally strong enough to put down the
grosser sentiments. All speakers know that they
must carry the audience with them or fail ; for here
the strongest human being is not sufficient unto himself. Oratory is eminently a social gift; and an

audience " *en rapport* " is as essential as the speaker
to a thoroughly successful effort.

The loyalty of Woman to womanhood is often
stronger than creeds, or rivalries, or personal ambi-
tions. In all these years I have never seen a woman
standing on our Woman's platform, who, when self-
love or personal feeling, however deep and of long
standing, has fairly come to be pitted against the
cause of Womanhood, has not put aside the personal
interest, in behalf of the wider interests of the sex.
This is saying a great deal ; for some pretty sharp
tests have arisen inevitably from time to time. If
any class of men have been so uniformly loyal to manhood, I have not so read history. Men have no
common cause like ours. Unless, hereafter, in some
new phases of development, it shall come to be suspected that Mrs. Farnham's theory is correct, and
men are the real inferiors of women ; and unless the
men are then put on trial to prove that they are not
deficient somewhere, they never can develop the
highest sympathies of sex, these broadest and most
impersonal of special social instincts,

IX.

In these brief papers I have several times referred to Dr. Brown-Séquard, because he is among the active physiologists of the day, and also, because, at the time, he was giving a course of lectures in Boston, stating some of the more curious and striking phenomena of the nervous system. These were printed by the New York *Tribune*, and scattered broadcast over the land. Taking up his last lecture, I was half startled to find his summary of the laws of health so exactly identical with those insisted on in this series on Sex and Work, that if the latter had not been written, and except the last, printed in advance, I could have believed myself unconsciously to have directly re-produced his "great rules of hygiene," as I now do consciously and with immense satisfaction. It will be profitable to ponder these important concluding paragraphs of a very remarkable course of lectures, from an authority equal, perhaps, to any in the world.

"There is, I repeat, no force in our system, other

than mere nerve force, for the transmission, that may come from the brain, as the seat of the imagination, the seat of emotion, and the seat of the will.

"I shall now add but a few words on the production and expenditure of nerve force. Nerve force is produced, as you know, through blood. It is a chemical force which is transformed there into nerve force. This nerve force accumulates in the various organs of the nervous system, in which it is formed during rest. But if rest is prolonged, then it ceases to be produced. Alteration takes place in the part which is not put to work. On the other hand, action, which is so essential to the production of nerve force, if prolonged, will exhaust force also, but produce a state distinct from that of rest. Rest will produce a lack of blood, while over-action may produce congestion. The great thing, therefore, is to have sufficient, but not excessive action.

"There is another law, which is, that we should not exercise alone one, two, or three of the great parts of the nervous system ; since thus we draw blood to those parts only, and the other parts of the body suffer. In the due exercise of all our organs lie the principal rules of hygiene. This view, you know, comes from a physician. But it is certainly true that the great rule of health is not to lay imagination aside. Imagination, on the contrary, is to be appealed to far more than we do, and this is one of the great conclusions that I hope young physicians will keep in mind.

"To conclude with these great rules of hygiene, I should say that we should not spend more than our means allow us. Many commit this fault. As before said, we should make an equal use of all our organs, and of the various parts of the nervous system. Those who employ the brain, suffer a great deal from inattention to this law.

"Lastly, there should be regularity as regards the time of meals, the time and amount of action, the time and amount of sleep—regularity in everything. It is very difficult indeed to obtain it. But there is in our nature more power than we know, and if we conform ourselves to the law of habit, things will soon go on without our meddling with them, and we come to be perfectly regular, although we perhaps had naturally a tendency not to be."

It is true that Dr. Brown-Séquard prescribes these rules for human beings, making no reference to Woman. But if the half of the race are to be considered as exceptions, undoubtedly he could not well have overlooked that important fact. We must conclude, therefore, that he has but one set of health rules for men and women, and that these may all be summed up in one; the habitual, moderate exercise of all the great, nervous centres, of which the brain is chief.

Many other persons have arrived at the same conclusion. Probably a majority among physicians, on reflection, would cheerfully consent to believe that good students, by a balanced exercise of brain and muscle, might become much healthier than day laborers. But the workman himself probably believes that study is akin to poison in its health-ruining effects; and this continues to be the favorite theory of the more studious multitude, who rejoice to believe that they and their learned friends can have the monopoly of that honorable and refined ailment, "too much brain work." It is a clear case of the influence of imagination which needs a pretty thorough reconstruction before it can be appealed to successfully in the interest of good health.

And what is "the type of intermittence" theory doing in this direction for the women? What, but, through the imagination of every anxious mother and every timid girl, converting healthful, daily regularity in time and amount of study, into a positive bane ; turning frightened women back from the habitual use of the one great nerve centre, without the due exercise of which there is no possibility of restoring them to vigorous and refined health. It is but just to remember that Dr. Clarke really believes in brain work for women, and that it is to the daily regularity type, the "persistent type" of study that he seriously objects. But "regularity in everything" is best promoted by conforming ourselves to the strict "law of habit," through which all the processes of good health will soon learn to go on comfortably "without our meddling with them." This, at least, is the hygienic teaching of Dr. Brown-Séquard ; a line of instruction which should do much to counteract the opposing influence.

If it is true that Nature, mindful of the welfare of

her little children, has endowed Woman—the mother —with a special structure and functions admirably adapted to enable her, far beyond man, to bear any unusual tax upon her energies, whether of underwork or of overwork, in one or in all directions; and if, in the fulfilment of her maternal relations, all the resources and the whole enormous elasticity of her nature is sometimes most severely taxed, then she, immeasurably more **than man,** can be benefited by thoroughly acquiring the habit of "regularity in everything." That power, more than we know, in her nature, can then help her in all emergencies, with incalculable advantage. A physique that has been strengthened by daily, regular exercise of all the great nervous centres, will then have its resources at command, and by the continued moderate use of all her powers, a woman may wonderfully aid her well-balanced constitution in avoiding all unhealthy functional disturbances.

Whoever else may object to this view of the subject, Dr. Clarke can hardly do so and still be logically consistent. He distinctly accepts some, and most undoubtedly accepts all the facts of special provision for continued feminine health. Then, is one who is provided with special helps and faculties towards anything to be regarded as less likely to attain it, than he who has no such provision? Or, because these special powers, like all others, are liable to disturbance, are they, therefore, to be held up as a normal source of disability, and their possessors warned off from exercising the common activities, alike available and desirable to them and to their less well endowed neighbors?

Why is it so difficult to believe, then, that at any and at every crisis which can arise in the healthy female life, regularity, but moderation in the exercise of all the great, nervous centres must be of immense gain? Organs already too much congested by any disturbed activity of their functions, will thus often be greatly relieved by some counter activity, and the balance restored. The whole system will be regulated by the orderly force of persistent habit.

Above all, when the mind is healthfully occupied, it finds less time and less temptation for the indulgence of exhausting, nervous anxiety, or for the culture of any form of painful sensation. The truest philosophy then, as well the most humane physiology, should join hands to enlist the power of imagination upon the right side of this question, and convince Woman that she has no right to be an invalid. A cure for the whole class of feminine ills which everybody is called on now, in pity, to deplore, will then be more than half achieved.

X.

We assume that study, properly performed, like all other natural exercise of our faculties, should be a direct and positive benefit to the health of Man or Woman. Why, then, are students so generally bloodless and without muscular strength?

Suppose the blacksmith should put his feet in the stocks, or steadily sit while working at his anvil, would he retain the health which he proverbially acquires? His arms might retain their disproportionate vigor till the body became gradually enfeebled; but such a regimen, persisted in, would probably end by making his strong right arm as powerless as that of any professional gentleman. Some balance of action is necessary in the exercise of one's functions or loss of vitality is inevitable. The exclusive use of any organ, though it should be of some help to all the others, can by no means wholly compensate for their disuse ; therefore, one who is a student merely, or too absorbingly, has no right to expect a vigorous physical system. Yet the same amount of study, supplemented by more muscular activity, might place him in a robust mental and physical condition.

To this unbalanced activity, is very generally added an exhausting, thoroughly improvident method of brain-work, which, though it may not be excessive in the aggregate, is yet so unwisely performed that the constitution becomes enfeebled through its influence. No amount of counteracting exercise can atone for study prolonged till the brain is over-exhausted—the drain upon it leaving its energies so prostrated that it has no power of prompt and healthful recuperation. Change and rest then are both used up as medicine to restore, not utilized as added strength to the whole system. I believe this to be much the most common mode by which study, in amount moderate enough if properly distributed, yet becomes enfeebling to the whole general constitution. One inordinately large meal, to last over for the whole twenty-four hours, would exactly parallel the prevailing tendency of a student's life. Then we talk of the injurious effects of study !

A woodchopper may continue healthfully at his work for many hours together ; but every hewer of thought will prolong his work at his peril. The more intense the action of his brain, the more rapidly exhausting ; the more absolute the requirement for frequent and complete relaxation. A steady rainfall will continue for hours or days unchecked, while the flash of lightning is momentary, yet equally effective in its work of clarifying the atmosphere. The subtler forces in Nature can accomplish more in minutes than their equivalents in months or years. We have only to remember that the swift, molecular motion of brain and nerve is to the cumbrous movement of the whole body, or one of its heavy members, as the flight of a sunbeam to the swing of the great earth in its orbit, to comprehend how much oftener and longer we need rest from brain-work than from any almost mechanical handicraft. Alas! for the student who will not leave his lessons unlearned, or the thinker who will not suffer his brightest thoughts to fall back into chaos, rather than exhaust the delicate living mechanism through which he is constrained to work.

But what right have we to assume that the temperate use of any of our faculties can be otherwise than strengthening to all the others? Every process in Nature is but some mode of work ; and if there is unity in the human constitution, male or female, the due use of all our functions, those highest in character kept most continually in exercise, must outline the noblest method of healthful self-development. Overwork is dwarfing to body and soul; but cultivated, habitual activity carries within itself perennial satisfaction and the assured renewal of every power brought into exercise.

At a New York reception given to Canon Kingsley, some one—I think that veteran worker and poet, Wm. C. Bryant—among other good wishes, desired for the distinguished Englishman the blessing of a long life. Canon Kingsley responded that he himself desired anything but that, indicating that he intended to work too diligently to dream of length of days as his portion.

As though the very best work, which he or any one else could normally accomplish, would not be the identical work which should tone both muscle and brain up to the very highest pitch of steady, persistent endurance ! As though health and long life were not the direct natural reward for the very highest work most fittingly accomplished, which lies within the scope of one's powers, physical and mental ! Suicide by overwork is not much more laudable than by the halter ; and such a sentiment from a Canon in the Established Church of England, and an apostle in the establishing church of muscular Christianity, is doubly reprehensible. *

Old age must be subject to its own pathetic weaknesses, which no human prudence can forestall ; but

---

* While the above is in press, word comes that all too soon Canon Kingsley's prophecy is fulfilled. Excessive work may have prepared the way for this mournful result, but it is connected with a pulmonary attack when in this country, and is another evidence of the sharp and decisive action of our excating climate. This event sadly emphasizes two points in our argument.

that mental power should ever fail in advance of the physical is pitiable ; that it would be impossible, if prolonged and fortified by judicious habitual exercise, it seems almost impious to deny. The food which nourishes the octogenarian is as fresh and young as that which builds up the frame of a little child, and thought is always young and immortal ; the failure lies wholly in the want of a mobile activity in the recipient. The only hope of warding off age, and counteracting its weaknesses must lie in co-operation with Nature, who secures all her ends through some form of movement or work.

Work ! work ! In nothing else is there hope for man, or beast, or vegetable, that would continue to live. If age would maintain its failing tissues in their utmost integrity, would eliminate the half-deadened matter which stiffens and clogs its activity, physical and psychical, there is but one class of means to this end, work ! Nature has no royal road. Work with every faculty of the mind and with every muscle of the body ; this will give the nearest approximation to perpetual, universal youth.

Society has tenderly constrained its favored wives

and daughters to reduce activity, especially all sensible, thoroughly inspiriting activity, to the lowest practicable rate. Then we wonder at the invalidism which comes on apace. But let every woman comprehend fully that inactivity is death! The laws of Nature are not to be set aside for our benefit. Our Father worketh hitherto, and we must work.

"THE BUILDING OF A BRAIN."

THIS new work of Dr. E. H. Clarke takes a new and higher point of departure than that in "Sex and Education" as its basis of argument. The former demanded a recurring interregnum in the school life of the girl ; the latter claims only the need for rest from "gymnastics, long walks, and such like ; " from "dancing, visiting, and similar offices," admitting that the ordinary home and school life may then "only be interfered with in exceptional cases." This new platform is broad enough for us all.

Claiming various modifications in the practical methods of carrying out the feminine health question, I desire to place myself fully and squarely upon this new vantage ground. The walks must only mean long walks; the gymnastics, violent or protracted gymnastics; the visiting, exciting social life —chiefly objectionable at all times—and the dancing must be of the prolonged party and ball-room variety. Then, every well-informed man and woman must heartily endorse Dr. Clarke's present position.

All severe study long continued, all exciting school examinations criminally prolonged to exhaustion may be cut off, also, with every other form of excess. They are all ruinous to the health of girls. But are they not about equally ruinous to the health of boys? Are the great majority of nervous American tourists, who are sent off every year to seek health in Europe, men or women? Report says that they are chiefly ministers, lawyers, business men. Let the public be offered a full and complete accumulation of facts, bearing upon all sides of the health and endurance questions, as between the two sexes, and I believe that it will be found that the women of this country, as a class, taking all ages into the account, are not greater invalids than the men. If a hundred Dr. Clarkes will ring out a clear note of warning against the high pressure system, which begins in our school life, but which ends nowhere, we may all thank God and take courage.

But the question still recurs: Will a course of

study, which is not too severe a tax upon the boy, prove perilous to the health of the girl of the same age? Let us understand that they are no more likely to learn lessons by exactly the same methods, than they are to approach any topic from the same standpoint. "The only difference between the sexes is sex;" but this is a difference even more comprehensive than Dr. Clarke seems to; admit for it so modifies every drop of blood in the veins, and every thought and act in the life, that one can only be made less masculine or less feminine through being maimed in limb or dwarfed in mind. For a woman to become coarse or unbalanced is not to become masculine! Sex must be something more fundamental than this. It must imply some differentiation in everything—even to every hair of the head. The microscope may be able to discern no difference between the brains of the sexes, yet there must be a difference all the same, else there can be no reliance upon logic, and nature's diverse methods of working, at some stage in every organism, must become a mockery.

Sex means differentiation in every process of

body and mind. The question is not : Can a girl study as many hours as a boy, equally without harm ? but it is : Can she obtain an equal mastery of the same school tasks without harm ? Certainly it is not yet indicated that she cannot. The whole existing body of data looks directly the other way.

In most of the mixed schools, the girls average a younger age than the boys, and yet they excel them in proficiency. Besides, they are more burdened with hurtful conventional and industrial duties, and are allowed a much less unfettered reactive activity. I am far from claiming that they need an equal *amount* of out-of-door exercise, or of any other form of energy. But doubtless they are in equal need of a similar balance of activities, mental and physical. Educators must learn to comprehend nature's differences in method !

It must be safe to act upon the principle of demanding equivalent results from each. As it is found that girls need the less stimulus, give them less. They generally study in separate rooms, even when reciting together. If girls require less practice in order to arrive at like facility in execution; if they

can memorize faster, or if they can find more direct
methods of reaching an equal comprehension of principles, any well instructed teacher accepting these
differences can allow for them in his requirements.
It only needs an extended application of common
sense in order to adjust all this without friction.
Every half-mature girl will be more than content to
do her studying in her own natural way, just as soon
as there can be a sincere withdrawal of the current
flippant charges against the feminine intellect, accus-
ing it of superficiality and inferiority, and confound-
ing its naturally quicker insight with vulgar "shrewd
guessing."

Both sexes must comprehend that science, as yet,
has no data that we can fall back upon. Physiology
and psychology, hygiene and medical science, all
alike confound woman with man, in everything except in her domestic characteristics. A womanhood
with a complexity of character and functions, if such
a type has been evolved in the world, is as yet undis-
covered by the scientific intellect. Or, if Deity created it in the beginning, theologians have never yet
recognized His handiwork. The higher education of

women must draw a long train of consequences in its wake. It requires a deeper reading of facts, a reconsideration of all the old data, from the bottom upwards; in a word, a new science—the science of Feminine Humanity. For this we must rely largely upon facts, to be slowly and carefully gathered, and to be still more slowly and guardedly lived, if there are not to arise some very painful mistakes.

But the experience of women must count for more here than the observation of the wisest men. Till the public has some real comprehension of the great problem to be solved, it can be expected to make only blundering progress towards its solution. Yet we must be safe in falling back upon the obvious first principle, that women can no more need a different class of mental food than they can need a different style of beef, mutton, and vegetables. A lady once told me she found it extremely difficult to take her meals alone habitually, and yet to continue in good health. Her explanation was this: By herself, she was at a loss how to graduate the amount of food which it was best to take. Appetite was often an uncertain guide. But if she could observe the amount taken by half a dozen others about her, she was able to strike a much more satisfactory average for herself.

So of the mental diet of the sexes. Whatever girls can appropriate easily, boys can be made to digest without detriment ; but any amount which will endanger the health of girls must be too great also for boys of the same age. Let the sexes work together, to be a mutual check and measure of each other, since Nature so evidently intended them to keep side by side from life's beginning to its latest goal.

I will close by bringing forward the main plank in Dr. Clarke's new platform, upon which we all stand together in the prime interest of the most healthful and most symmetrical brain-building :

" The method that builds a man's builds also a woman's brain. But this identity of method in cerebral architecture, which requires that every organ and every function in both sexes should have appropriate development and exercise, as a part of brain-building, implies, or rather necessitates, a difference in education between the sexes, just so far as there is a difference in organization between them, and no farther."

THE TRIAL BY SCIENCE.

THE co-educational discussion probably reached its climax in 1874. "Drs. Clarke and Maudsley and the millions of social conservatives to whose dumb instincts they have given utterance," are no longer standard-bearers in the contest. No coming spring will see every paper and magazine budding into articles and paragraphs on the subject, till their number is like the leaves in a thick wood. Book after book : *The Education of American Girls, Sex and Education, No Sex in Education,* still remain as the contributions of earnest women to a question in which they must continue to feel the most vital interest.

The public has instinctively recognized and emphasized a point made by the *Westminster Review* in one of the last and ablest contributions to a discussion which agitated both sides of the Atlantic : "We are constrained to admit that the doctresses certainly can appeal to specific personal experiences bearing directly on the question—experiences capable of outweighing a vast amount of the mere reasoning and information at second-hand of their professional brethren ; moreover, the doctresses have facilities of intimate and confidential communications from and discussions with their own sex on the subject, yielding information likely to be more copious, more varied, and more exact than is the information obtainable by the doctors.   And it must be added that, viewing this information in the light shed upon it by their own personal experience, they are likely to appreciate it in all its bearings more accurately than men can do.   It thus appears that, *cæteris paribus*, the opinion of Doctress Garrett-Anderson and of Doctress Putnam-Jacobi is likely, precisely by virtue of their womanhood, to be more correct, and therefore more reliable, than the opinion of Drs. Clarke and Maudsley."

Women "have special knowledge of the subject in question." It is one which must be largely tested by experience—by the experience of generation succeeding generation ; and the interest in it, though perhaps coming less freely to the surface, must deepen and broaden in the future, suffering no real diminution. Every educator of either sex, quickened by throbs of the public pulse, like the Editor of the *Popular Science Monthly*, must ask whether existing inequalities are "accidental and removable," or whether they are "radical and permanent, and belong to the very constitution of the sexes." Data enough must be accumulated on one side or the other to fully determine whether or not Nature has entailed on one sex disabilities which are not offset and equalled by similar disabilities in the other.

Valuable as are many of the contributions towards a solution of this question, yet it cannot be regarded as scientifically settled. Reasoners who arrive at kindred conclusions can still hold to opposite physiological premises. Thus, the *Westminster Review* rejects the theory that "the reproductive apparatus of woman uses the blood as one of its agents of elimination of effete and used material," on the ground that the "spontaneous depletion has nothing in common with the nature of true secretion." But is not effete matter eliminated through the breath, especially in a disordered state of the system ; and is that in the nature of a true secretion ? Are the moisture or the carbonic acid of the expired breath true secretions ?

But this is not a question to be determined by analogies. It can be settled only by the most careful and extended chemical tests. Mere analogy seems to indicate that a stream flowing into every part of a perpetually wasting system and giving it the materials for repair, will receive from it such *debris* as is not immediately eliminated by special organs ; and analogy would further lead us to suppose that Nature in her depleting process will seek, incidentally at least, to eliminate impurities. But this would be an advantage, not a disadvantage, on the side of woman.

A discussion half popular, half scientific, has many disadvantages to contend against. Yet it is evidently to the popular element of agitation—to the raising of present practical issues—that woman is indebted mainly for the attention which has been bestowed upon her by modern science. It is now generally admitted that it would be as futile to expect the Bible to settle her position in the community as to expect it to settle the details of domestic service, or the exact process of the creation of the world. Hence, if she applies for admission to Harvard, Harvard can offer its most humane denial in the name of Physiology. If she applies for an introduction to some of the privileges and responsibilities of English politics, England, speaking by the mouth of her latest philosopher, replies in the name of Psychology : " *So that, if any change is made, we may make it knowing what we are doing.*" If it is a question of medical education and recognition, from the high authority of his scientific pinnacle, Prof. Huxley announces that he finds no evidence in proof that superior women are the equals of superior men, yet they are clearly entitled to compete with inferior men. Prof. Goldwin Smith, drawing his conclusions from two continents, and speaking for the benefit of both, also discusses the question from a purely practical point of view. The opinions of our scientific countrymen, generally as fragmentary as the bird-like tracks in the Connecticut sandstone, have to be determined by comparison and inference. Apparently they have not reached unanimous conclusions.

The editor of the *Popular Science Monthly,* com-

paring John Stuart Mill and Herbert Spencer as philosophers, refers to the unlike methods of these two
eminent thinkers in their treatment of the Woman
Question. Prof. Youmans claims that Mr. Mill might
have written his treatise on *The Subjection of Woman*
two thousand years ago, while Mr. Spencer has
grounded his conclusions on principles of modern science which were beyond the reach of past generations.

This criticism seems to be entirely just. But it
must be remembered that these two investigators belonged in reality to two different generations. By
education and acquired habits of thought, Mr. Mill
was as old as his own father. It is the more remarkable, therefore, that, using the older, speculative
methods, he yet reached conclusions of a modern type ; while Mr. Spencer, by modern scientific
reasoning, has succeeded in grounding himself anew
upon the moss-grown foundations of ancient dogma.

Yet it is to the most rigid scientific methods of
investigation that we must undoubtedly look for a
final and authoritative decision as to woman's legitimate nature and functions. Whether we approve or
disapprove, we must be content, on this basis, to

settle all questions of fact pertaining to the feminine economy. In these days, science is testing every thing pertaining to this world and even reaching out towards the next. In physiology, in psychology, in politics, in all forms of social life, it is to Nature as umpire—to Nature interpreted by scientific methods, that we most confidently appeal.

But science has not yet made the feminine constitution and its normal functions a prolonged and careful study. No investigator has attempted conclusively to determine the relative energy or endurance of the sexes from sufficient and carefully recorded data. Science possesses no body of facts quantitative or qualitative, upon which it can be entitled to make an estimate with any assurance of its correctness. Thus, when physiologists discuss the influence of sex in education, they make no attempt to indicate a related series of organic and functional differentiations such as would necessarily lead us to the conclusion that the same kind and amount of study will be more injurious to one sex than to the other. So far as appears, this conclusion is based on nothing more sure than a "great probability" or preconception.

Current physiology seems to be grounded on the assumption that woman is undersized man, with modified organs and special but temporary functions, which like all other more or less abnormal activities are a direct deduction from the normal human energy. When this being, so varied from the masculine type, has been studied as to these variations, then all that is over and above these is simply man—nothing more ; but something less, as an exhausted potato is less by every sprout which has grown and been rubbed off from its dozens of germinal centres.

A *psychology* based on such a *physiology* can be no more scientific.   It is not likely to rise even into the higher regions of psychological theorizing.   It accepts the traditions which are allied to its authority. In the case of Mr. Spencer, even his ruling tendencies as an evolutionist have not been able to carry him a single step beyond.   He accepts the popular, traditional estimate ; but by masterly philosophical explanations, the philosopher dignifies the tradition ; planting it firmly upon what he claims to be an unshaken scientific basis.

Mr. Darwin in his line of thought has done the

same ; he also has come by a fresh pathway to the old conclusion, and, building upon a mountain of evidence over which he has faithfully toiled in defence of another hypothesis, he announces authoritatively : " *Thus* man has ultimately become superior to woman." He adds with delicious sympathy : " It is, indeed, fortunate that the law of the equal transmission of characters to both sexes has commonly prevailed throughout the whole class of mammals ; otherwise it is probable that man would have become as superior in mental endowments to the woman, as the peacock is in ornamental plumage to the peahen."

When these two illustrious names, eminent in science, both thinkers who have more profoundly influenced the opinions of the civilized world than perhaps any other two living men—when these two, endorsed by other world-wide authorities, are joined in assigning the mete and boundary of womanly capacities ; and when the physiologists assume to interpret physical limitations, announcing authoritatively to the world that the weaker sex is unfitted constitutionally for persistent work, physical or mental, it is time to recognize the fact that the " irrepressible woman question" has already taken a new scientific departure. Woman herself must speak hereafter, or forevei holding her peace, consent meekly to crown herself with these edicts of her inferiority. She must consent to put in evidence the results of her own experience, and to develope the scientific basis of her differing conclusions. Doubtless this must involve also her consent to meet criticism, and to meet, if she must, the evidence of her incapacity, and of her unfitness for the work undertaken. If Nature has so decreed, she must consent to see her positions annihilated; and even to feel herself humiliated for her presumption.

But there can be no humiliation! A thinking dog might or might not over-estimate the capabilities of canine nature; but no humane being could respect him the less for attempting to vindicate the capacities of his kind. Humanity could not visit him with added scorn because of his too ambitious claims to respectful consideration.

A belief in the more rapid and subtle action of the feminine mind, as a balance to the massiveness and weight of the sterner masculine type, is a spontaneous growth from modern culture. Few persons may be able to offer sufficient evidence of its truth; thousands may accord to it merely a courteous but unmeaning significance, yet the fact remains: that woman's intuitional, affectional, and moral traits are rapidly approaching par in current general estimation.

It was authoritatively decreed from time immemorial that man is the superior, physically, mentally, legally, and by Divine ordinance. This position remained unshaken in the early days of brute supremacy and dominant muscular strength. Now it is universally controverted. The higher the grade of culture in any community, the more nearly does woman gain recognition as the equal and peer of man. Mr. Herbert Spencer has very effectively used the argument of a presumptive evidence against any opinion which arose in an ignorant and barbarous era; but which is called in question in more enlightened times, and discredited by evidences accessible to us only after the race has made very considerable progress in science and philosophy. Nothing, therefore, but the most thoroughly sifted and undeniable scientific evidence, can now make us cling to the old dogma of feminine inferiority. The old theory of a righteous vassalage of one sex to the other, must be shown to us endorsed by the clear sign-manual of Nature herself ; else we must continue to believe that equal halves make the perfect whole.

When Dr. Clarke's first educational treatise was published, the Ladies' Benevolent Associations began to devise the most feasible and humane schemes for importing the providentially waiting Chinamen, with the view of transferring to their masculine shoulders the duties of child nurses, cooks, washwomen, and housekeepers ! They comprehended that girls reared under the new regimen might become mothers ; yet it would be hopeless to expect them to sustain the un-remitted burdens of domestic detail ! Now this movement is arrested, since Dr. Clarke, in his "*Building of a Brain*," concedes to the average woman the possibility of continued good health while engaged in the unremitted duties of ordinary home and school life.

Fortified by this significant change in recent opinion, I venture the more resolutely to suggest that all the learned authorities who have decided the intellectual inferiority of Woman from scientific data, will yet find that their conclusions require modification from the introduction of unforeseen elements into their premises.

There is no adequate Psychology of Womanhood. If Mr. Spencer had completed his entire *Sociology*, it is not probable that he either would or could have brought together sufficient data to enable us to determine whether, in all ages and nations, the aggregate amounts of masculine and feminine energy actually expended have or have not been equivalent factors. The woman of the past is little known in history. Her mental life has left almost no record of itself. The motives and influences under which she has acted can only be inferential. Even the present woman must be tested more by *physiology* than by *psychology*. We cannot directly compare mind with mind. Nor can we fairly estimate the intellectual work of men and women in comparison, unless we first determine that the work was done under equivalent conditions equally favorable to each. But such conditions do not exist ; they have never existed hitherto. Therefore the earliest solution of the question must probably come through quantitative physical data. The mind works through the body. We must first establish estimates of the relative amounts of energy expended in thought, in feeling, in muscular action, and in reproductive functions, and must approach some standard of comparison as to the characteristic differences of male and female in all these respects ; and we must reach some estimate as to their relative powers of appropriating and of using force, before there can be even an approximate basis for scientific comparison either of the physical or of the psychical characters of the sexes.

One theory is, that man is and always has been the superior ; the other, that woman is and always has been man's full equivalent. He has always largely used and economized his powers as a thinking being : she, fettered by conventionality, has largely suffered hers to run to waste. Whichever theory is true, science can have no right to announce as " physiological truth," that because " women exhale smaller quantities of carbonic acid relatively to their weights, than men do," therefore that, " the evolution of energy is relatively less as well as absolutely less," unless it is prepared to show that there are no other modifying influences which can be fairly supposed to affect the result. Physiology must embrace the aggregate of physical characters in its estimate; Psychology must embrace the aggregate of psychical powers, and the real complexity of the question must be fairly apprehended. This will be done in this generation or in the next.

THE END.

DATE DUE

GAYLORD			PRINTED IN U.S.A.